THE **BEST STORY** OF **YOUR LIFE**

JOSEPH ANFUSO

Keep running The race!
Heb. 12:1

This book is dedicated to my children,
Heather, Ryan and Kate.

"We must be willing to let go of the life we've planned to have the life that is waiting for us."

— E.M. Forster

"God rewrote the text of my life when I opened the book of my heart to His eyes."

— 2 Samuel 22:25 MSG

Acknowledgments

Thanks to...

Karen, my closest collaborator, most constructive critic and best friend.

Heather Baker, Donna Tallman, Nick Harrison, Danah Behbehani, Katy Crane, Pam Lagielski, Jane Tuck, Jim Andrew and Lindsay Holmes for reading early drafts of this book, and offering their valuable feedback.

Beth Jusino whose editing brought added clarity and polish to the finished product.

Brad and Chris Fenison at Pediment Publishing for their expert craftsmanship and generous support.

Hans Bennewitz for his innovative cover design.

Tim Ainley for his help compiling the photo section.

The Forward Edge IHQ Team for allowing me to escape for a few weeks to put my thoughts on paper.

All those whose stories are told in these pages. Thank you for saying "yes" to God's unfolding plans for your lives.

What Others are Saying
About *The Best Story of Your Life*

"Once again, Joe Anfuso transcends traditional offerings in Christian literature with an immensely readable book that both regular churchgoers and the 'seekers' among us will enjoy. Joe's remarkable life story, his honesty, and his compassion for everyday people make The Best Story of Your Life *a powerful testament—and tool—for growing your faith.*"

— Pete Ferryman, Anchor, Good Day Oregon, KPTV Fox 12

....

"Proverbs 16:9 says: 'The mind of man plans his way but the LORD directs his steps.' Living each day in anticipation of God's intervention is the way every follower of Jesus ought to live! In his new book, The Best Story of Your Life, Joe Anfuso masterfully captures the wonder and amazement that can well up in our hearts when we learn to cease striving and begin joyfully watching as Jesus writes His story in and through us! As you read Joe's book, get ready for your own adventure!"

— Phil Colmer, Founding Pastor, Solid Rock Church

....

"Joseph Anfuso's compelling new book gives us eyes to see how God is uniquely at work in our lives, powerfully leading each of us toward a glorious destiny."

— Rich Stearns, President, World Vision US, author *The Hole in Our Gospel*

"How do you respond when life takes a turn you weren't expecting? In The Best Story of Your Life *Joseph Anfuso encourages Christ followers to respond to unforeseen circumstances with faith and obedience. Read this book, and begin to discover your destiny in Christ."*

— Kevin Palau, President, Luis Palau Association

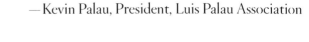

"Refreshingly honest and transparent, Joe Anfuso's new book shows how God uses unforeseen and sometimes unwelcome circumstances to continually draw us to Himself. I encourage you to read this book!"

— Ben Crane, PGA Tour golfer

"I am a follower of Christ—or at least I claim to be. In every day life I often wonder where God is present. Joseph Anfuso in his new book, The Best Story of Your Life, *reminds us that each day we are met with 'God-ordained circumstances' where God is at work. Whether in the earthquake in Haiti or a pub in Ireland, our awareness of the presence of God in those moments, and our resulting choices, determine our destiny. This book is at the same time encouraging and challenging. It's a message that followers of Christ need to contemplate and act upon. If you want to find your God-ordained 'story' read* The Best Story of Your Life."

— Robin Baker, President, George Fox University

"Standing at a central point in our understanding of the meaning of having a spiritual life and path is Joseph Anfuso and this book. Unless we can explore through our experiences of life what God's plan actually means, and how

God is working inside our concrete circumstances, we will be in good measure left confused and unsure of what we are up to. Anfuso's central concept of 'serendestiny' is his way of sharing his own deepest grasp of this mystery of creative fidelity between God and human beings. Pick up this book and read, and you will hear more than this author addressing you."

— Father Richard "Rick" H. Ganz, SJ, Vice President for Community Relations and University Chaplain, Marylhurst University

....

"Joseph Anfuso knows life is as hard as the ground we walk on. Which is why his book, The Best Story of Your Life, is such a timely and refreshing gift. Joseph's story is a much-needed oasis on the ever-challenging road of real life and faith. I absolutely loved this book. What surprised me is how personally it spoke to me...very timely, insightful and helpful. Read this inspiring book and experience, as I did, transforming moments of 'serendestiny' along the way."

— Kip Jacob, Senior Pastor, SouthLake Church

....

"This is a wonderful book for those of us who want to do God's will, but are sometimes puzzled by the seemingly haphazard way God works. In reality, God has a destiny for us that's only revealed as we respond in faith to the circumstances of our lives. Joseph Anfuso helps us see through the mist of confusion to apprehend God's greater plan for us."

— Nick Harrison, senior editor at Harvest House Publishers and author of Magnificent Prayer

"'I'm not in charge' is one of the most difficult, sobering and adventurous truths you will ever learn! The Christian life is not a robotic activity that requires no human response. While God is in charge, He also searches for passion, rewards faith and loves risk takers. With this in mind, I commend to you the musings of a dear man of God called to infuse destiny in the lives of his readers."

—James W Goll, President, Encounters Network
and Prayer Storm, bestselling author

....

"Like the author, I've traveled the world seeking ways to serve the poor. How God molds us into servants He can use—whatever His call on our lives might be—is a process we can't fully anticipate or make happen on our own. Highly personal yet universally relevant, this powerful, well-written book will inspire you to discover and pursue your own God-given destiny. A must read!"

—Ron Post, Founder and Former President, Medical Teams
International and Co-Founder of Mission Increase Foundation

....

"I commend to you this 'Psalm of Joseph.' The Psalms in Scripture are creative, written expressions of biblical truth through the grid of life experience. They lead us to praise God and instruct us. This 'Psalm of Joseph' does the same. There are books designed to tell a story. There are books designed to instruct. Joe has done a masterful job of showing how his personal story, and those of others, interact with and illustrate biblical truth. But it doesn't stop there. I found two things happening to me as I read. First, I found myself thanking God 'for His unfailing love and His wonderful deeds for men' (see Ps 107:8, 15, 21, 31). Second, I found myself growing 'in grace and the knowledge of our Lord and Savior, Jesus Christ' (see 2 Peter 3:18). As you approach The Best Story of

Your Life, *prepare yourself for both an entertaining and profitable read.*"
— Dennis Fuqua, President, International Renewal Ministries,
Author, *Living Prayer* and *United and Ignited*

....

"*This is a wonderful book of story-telling presented in an easy-to-understand and endearing fashion. Through the process of self-discovery, Joe shares remarkably personal stories from his peripatetic journeys around the world to remind us to be faithful to our Lord and Savior regardless of our circumstances or the curveballs thrown our way. He reminds us that God is in control of our lives and calls us to simply be obedient. More than a memoir,* The Best Story of Your Life *allows the reader to learn and make sense of his or her own life's journey in the context of 'serendestiny,' that is, discovering one's destiny by responding with faith and obedience to unforeseen, and sometimes unwelcome circumstances.*"
— John Castles, Trustee, Murdock Charitable Trust

....

"*Some three decades after founding Forward Edge International, Joe Anfuso is the first-mate on a three-masted schooner, with God's Spirit blowing in its sails. Like Joe, I've discovered the thrills of following Jesus into the unknown. Now, it's your turn to read this powerful, fast-paced book and gladly embrace your own God-scripted destiny. Enjoy!*"
— David Sanford, Special Representative of the
President, Corban University

....

"*I've known Joe for eighteen years now. His relationship to my life has been defining; or as he would put it in this book, 'serendestinous.' Joe's new book is not so much an intellectual exercise as a journey with him to the heart of a supernatural Father, and His outrageous love for us and a very broken world. Enjoy!*

—Major John Greholver, Salvation Army

....

"*Joe Anfuso's new book,* The Best Story of Your Life, *teaches us that we need to watch for the unexpected ways God shows up in our lives, and with discernment, act intentionally in Christ when that happens. In his first book,* Message in a Body, *Joe tells his personal story and faith journey. In this latest book, he gives us a spiritual playbook, based on his own personal encounters with God and those of others, that will help you better understand, watch for and respond with faith to God's unlikely interventions in your life. A must-read book!*"

—Donald L. Krahmer, Jr., Co-chair, Business and Technology Practice, Schwabe Williamson & Wyatt, PC

....

"*With deep honesty, Joe Anfuso shares his passion to see people experience the life only a loving God could dream up and deliver to those willing to respond. Get ready to step into your own 'God-sized' adventure and discover why you're really here!*"

—Ron Frey, President, Frey Resource Group

"Joe Anfuso begins by defining "serendestiny," a term he coined, as a way of explaining how God intervenes in our lives and directs our steps in ways we can never imagine. By the time you finish his new book, you will be acutely aware that God loves you and has a plan for your life. A perfect plan! In reading The Best Story of Your Life *my eyes would suddenly well with tears as I sensed God speaking to my heart about how He has worked behind the scenes in my life. Joe's honesty and open confession about his own struggles to discover God's will for his life somehow worked to lower my defense shields. I ended up receiving a timely message where I am in life that I didn't even know I needed to hear. I am greatly encouraged."*

—Dave Andersen, President, Andersen Construction

....

"When we were younger, even reading Joe's postcards from random corners of the earth captivated me. Joe still chooses to see firsthand what most of us can barely imagine. And when he writes about these experiences he paints unforgettable pictures with words you'll never forget. Every time I ask where he's been I end up crying, either for joy or sadness. But in the end I'm always inspired to be the person God created me to be. Perhaps that's Joe's greatest gift."

—Francis Anfuso, Co-Senior Pastor, The Rock of Roseville

....

*"*The Best Story of Your Life *is a superb reminder to lean into God's 'bright but unknowable agenda' for our lives."*

—Chad Hayward, Executive Director, Accord Network

"*Reading* The Best Story of Your Life *felt like having a 'buddy-fare' ticket and traveling with the author on a riveting globe-hopping, spiritual adventure. The founder of Forward Edge International takes us to some of the places he's traveled as a rapid-response, missions man: Ireland, Haiti, India, Nepal, Albania and Brooklyn to name a few. Bracingly honest and vividly written,* The Best Story of Your Life *succeeds in not only bringing us along on some incredible adventures, but outfitting us as fellow travelers in the discovery of God's unique plans for our own lives.*"

—Jim Andrew, Senior Pastor, The Mission

....

"*Has God given a vision for you to pursue, or simply a continual longing for something only He can bring into being? Me, too! But after reading* The Best Story of Your Life, *I want to quit grabbing the pencil out of God's Hand as He graciously writes my next chapter!*"

—Bill MacLeod, Founder, Mission ConneXion

....

"*Joe Anfuso has written a book which captures the poignancy of how God allows our lives to intersect with His grand purposes in ways that are both dramatic and ordinary. Joe has an important global perspective from which he sees God painting profound truth on the canvas of our lives.*"

—Dr. Mac Pier, President, The NYC Leadership Center

PREFACE

I ONCE HEARD A FITNESS DOCTOR share the secret of his good health. "Every morning I get up at 6:05 and do seven minutes of yoga," he explained. "It's a daily reminder that I can control my future destiny."

What the doctor meant, of course, was that he could choose good habits that helped keep him healthy. True enough. But something else in the doctor's remark stood out to me as remarkably untrue: the notion that he could control his destiny.

It's an attractive idea. Wouldn't life be easier if we could pre-design our futures however we saw fit? Think of the pain and inconvenience we could avoid! All we'd need was a vision of our preferred future—what we believed would be best for us—and enough discipline and "good habits" to bring that vision to pass.

The truth, however, is that we have little control of how our life unfolds. Factors beyond our control invariably intervene. Accidents happen. Illness strikes. Family members bless us—or hurt us. Many life experiences happen in spite of us, not because of us. In the famous words of Scottish poet Robert Burns: "The best laid [plans] of mice and men oft go awry."

Does this mean that we're mere spectators in this life—or worse, victims? No. It means that fulfilling our destinies often has less to do with our pre-conceived plans than with our responses to circumstances we do not anticipate or seek—circumstances over which we have no real control.

For the believer, trusting that God is orchestrating these circumstances—that He is "working all things together for good"[1]—can be challenging, especially when those circumstances are tragic and seemingly unfair. *Are You really there, Lord?* we may start to wonder. Gradually, we may even start subscribing to a "watchmaker" view of God, which explains suffering like this: God made the world, but after that He lost interest, leaving us alone to fend for ourselves.

While most Christ followers would deny having doubts about God's involvement in their lives, there's a human tendency to become spiritually complacent over time. Rather than experiencing life with childlike wonder, we easily settle into safe and predictable routines—practices and mindsets that give us the illusion of control. For Christians, this often includes theological or religious routines: spiritual disciplines, firmly-held doctrinal beliefs and well-intentioned acts of service. The idea that we can put God in a box, or that we can please Him by doing "all the right things," becomes a shield against the pain of disappointment and the discomfort of not having answers to our questions.

But God is not fettered by our imperfect belief systems or limited understanding of who He is and how He's supposed to behave. He is God. He can show up for us—or not show up—as

---

1. Romans 8:28

He so wills. And when we trust in Him, rather than in our finite understanding of Him, we are poised to experience Him— wherever, however and whenever He chooses to appear.

The inescapable reality for all of us, even the doctor mentioned above, is that none of us can control our destinies. We can, however, control our choices. And those choices will ultimately determine the story of our lives.

The book you are about to read is not a "how-to" book. There are no "7 steps to finding your destiny" or fool-proof formulas for living a successful, God-honoring life. I have simply presented some of the truths and ideas I've learned along the way, and offered "discussion starters" so you can join with other readers to share your own experiences, questions and insights. You may also .

May God's Spirit guide you into Truth, and—as you respond with humility, faith and obedience to whatever circumstances He ordains for you—discover and embrace the best story of your life.

Joseph Anfuso, September, 2012
joseph@forwardedge.org

JOSEPH ANFUSO

1

FUNGI

"The only way a servant can remain true to God is to be ready for the Lord's surprise visits. This readiness will not be brought about by service, but through expecting Christ at every turn. This sense of expectation will give our life the attitude of childlike wonder He wants it to have."

— Oswald Chambers

FEBRUARY, 2002

I FIRST ENCOUNTERED FUNGI THE DOLPHIN in the pages of a book—the *Lonely Planet* guide for Ireland. It wasn't an actual encounter, of course, just two paragraphs on pages 347 and 348. It was enough to make me want to meet him, though. So Karen and I set out from Dingle following the directions on page 348:

"From Dingle take the Tralee road and turn right down a lane about 1.5 km from the Esso garage. The turning is easy to miss so look for a set of whitish gateposts beside the lane. At the end of the lane is a tiny parking space (remember that the farmer needs access to his fields). Walk along the sea wall towards the old tower and you'll come to the harbour mouth."

I was acclimated by now to driving on the "wrong" side of the road, but with the steering column also on the wrong side, I was in a better position than Karen to savor the passing landscape, a postcard of mist-shrouded cottages accented by small groves of alder and oak. At last we came to what looked like whitish gateposts, and I spun our Ford Fiesta into a narrow dirt alley flanked by open fields. After bouncing along for a minute or two we came to a slight widening in the alley, which I presumed to be the "parking space." There were no other cars or people around, just a single cow that looked briefly in our direction, then calmly resumed its grazing.

"I love Ireland," Karen said, her green eyes smiling. "Thanks so much for bringing me here."

Our Ireland trip was my gift to Karen for our 25th wedding anniversary. Irish on both sides (her maiden name was Brennan), Karen seemed right at home on the Emerald Isle, her quick wit and cheery demeanor mirroring much of the local populace. Though not an avid traveler, Karen had taken to Ireland like a rose to sunshine. So had I.

From the moment we arrived, in fact, our journey seemed

to morph into a kind of fairy tale. We were still in the airport, filling out paperwork at the Avis rental-car counter, when an elderly man in a wool fedora and tweed jacket approached the counter.

"Can you direct me to the WC?" the old man asked in a thick Irish accent, using the European term for restroom.

"It's at the far end of the terminal," the clerk responded, pointing indifferently to his left.

A weary grimace fell across the old man's face.

"Ah, isn't it *always* like that?" he muttered.

As the old man ambled off, he seemed the very embodiment of Ireland—a nation which had borne its share of hardships with sad, yet mirthful, resignation. But he also reminded me of a more personal topic that I'd been thinking a lot about lately: how we respond to the hands life deals us.

Karen and I spent just two days in Dublin, barely enough time to view the Book of Kells[2] and take in a play at the Abbey Theater. It was the West Coast of Ireland we wanted to see most. Everything I'd heard and read about that part of the country intrigued me.

We were not disappointed. After a surprisingly short drive from Dublin to Galway, we headed south for the Dingle Peninsula, the tip of which was the closest point in Europe to America. It was in Dingle—a fishing community at the base of the peninsula—that we hoped to see Fungi, the lone dolphin

---

2. A beautifully illustrated manuscript of the four Gospels dating to the seventh and eighth centuries.

who'd settled years earlier in Dingle Bay. But before we got to Dingle, we stopped in Doolin, a tiny coastal town famed for its traditional Irish music.

We arrived at dusk, settled into our bed and breakfast, and headed for one of the town pubs, a 300-year-old establishment named Gus O'Connor's. The atmosphere inside was electric: locals and out-of-town visitors all gathered around long, lacquered tables, sipping their pints of Guinness while a band of musicians played feverishly in one corner. The sound of flutes, fiddles and uilleann pipes echoed off the walls. I loved it.

We'd barely sat down when a local Irishman with one leg and a thick white beard pulled up a chair at our table. After leaning his crutches on the wall behind his chair, he nodded politely in our direction, then turned toward the musicians without saying a word. I was intrigued.

"Can I buy you a Guinness?" I asked after a few minutes.

"No thanks," the old man replied. "I've lost too many friends to the drink."

During the conversation that followed, Karen and I learned that our new tablemate was a retired fisherman, a Doolin native, and a musician of sorts.

"What instrument do you play?" I asked.

"I don't play an instrument," he said. "I sing."

I was about to inquire if he sang in public when he rose from the table, remounted his crutches and hobbled toward the band. There'd been a break in the music, and the sound of fiddles was replaced by the chatter of beer-swilling patrons. On reaching the musicians, the old man whispered something into the fiddle player's ear, then stepped toward one of the microphones that dangled on wires from the pub's ceiling. The band struck up again, and the old man began to sing.

> *"I skimmed across Blackwater*
> *without once submerging*
> *onto the banks of an urban morning..."*

I was mesmerized. There was something about the timbre of the old man's voice and the boldness of his presentation that made his song more like a proclamation than a ditty in a bar. It wasn't until the second verse, though, that I realized the subject of his tune.

> *"And he, like a ghost beside me...goes down with the*
> *ease of a dolphin...*
> *and emerges...unlearned, unchained, unharmed.*
> *For he is the perfect creature, natural in every feature,*
> *And I am the geek with the alchemist's stone."*

I leaned toward Karen and whispered excitedly, "I think he's singing about *Jesus*, Karen. Listen to the chorus."

> *"One bright, blue rose outlives all those.*
> *Two thousand years, and so it goes.*
> *To ponder his death, and his life eternally."*[3]

---

3. *Bright Blue Rose* by Jimmy McCarthy

Marveling at the improbability of a one-legged fisherman singing about Jesus in an Irish pub, I thought of how God had the habit of showing up in my life when and where I least expected Him. I sensed that my time in Ireland was becoming more than just a colorful vacation—though that would have been enough. God was trying to reveal something to me, though what it was I could not yet fully discern.

The next morning Karen and I continued our journey southward to the Dingle Peninsula. Less "touristy" than other parts of Ireland, the peninsula was magnificent, with black-rock cliffs sloping down toward mile after mile of foaming surf; green hillsides dotted with quaint, stone farmhouses and long-haired sheep; and flocks of seagulls floating above barren islands just offshore. It was no wonder that two motion pictures—*Ryan's Daughter* and *Far and Away*—had been filmed on the Dingle Peninsula.

About halfway to Dingle, we came across a cluster of stone igloos scattered along the hillside, facing the sea. We pulled off the road to examine them more closely. According to a sign, the beehive huts had been built by seventh-century monks who'd fled the chaos of barbarian raids on the Continent. "In the depths of the Dark Ages," the sign read, "it was monks like these who kept literacy alive in Europe."

Squatting shoulder to shoulder inside one of the huts, Karen and I marveled at the resilience of these ancient believers.

I wonder if Christians today could respond to persecution the way they did? I mused, aware that some new and weighty revelation was still forming in my heart. *How we respond to life's hardships is more important than we realize.*

After driving all day, Karen and I arrived in Dingle and headed for the harbor. After we parked beside the curious cow, we found ourselves trudging along a moss-covered sea wall that led to the harbor mouth. On our right was Dingle Bay; on our left, a rocky hillside crowned by what appeared to be the turret of an ancient castle. *That must be the "the old tower,"* I thought.

"You think we'll see him?" Karen whispered, her eyes fixed on the mouth of the harbor. I said nothing. In general I was an optimist, but sometimes shielded myself from disappointment by lowering my expectations.

A thin mist rolled across the bay, and the smell of peat hung heavy in the air. At last we came to a small promontory that stretched out into the harbor like a natural pier.

Several minutes passed, our solitude punctuated only by the blinking of the Dingle lighthouse and the rhythmic splatter of tiny waves against the shoreline.

Suddenly, the stillness was shattered by Karen's shout. "There he is! There he is!"

I spun around in the direction of Karen's gaze, and what I saw took my breath away. Just twenty or thirty yards offshore, Fungi soared above the water like a Fourth-of-July spinner. Karen and I were speechless. Yes, we'd read about this dolphin who accompanied local fishermen out to sea each morning, then returned with them to the harbor at dusk. But we never thought we'd *see* him, especially not a stone's throw away!

No sooner had Fungi disappeared beneath the water when a large, middle-aged man—a local farmer, I presumed—strolled up the path.

"You could come here a thousand times and not see him do that!" the man barked, his beet-red nose and blue eyes beaming in the twilight. "My name's John Fitzgerald," he said, reaching out to shake my hand. "Where you folks from?"

"New York, originally," Karen replied. "We live in Washington now...the state, not the capital."

"Oh, dear," the man said, the smile on his face dissolving. "Please accept my condolences. Sometimes you wonder what this world is coming to." It was just five months since 9/11, and any mention of New York, whether in the States or abroad, tended to prompt sympathy.

"It was a terrible tragedy," I said. "But Ireland's had its own share of troubles."

"True enough," the farmer said. "We're all born to trouble, I'm afraid."

After a few more pleasantries, we said our goodbyes, the old man continuing on up the trail and Karen and I returning to our car.

That night, as I lay beside Karen, I could not stop thinking about Fungi, or the metaphor for Jesus in the one-legged Irishman's song: a dolphin. Odd as it sounds, my thoughts drifted back to a college course I'd taken on nineteenth-century American literature. One of the books we'd read was *Moby Dick*, and the professor had explained that while Ahab saw the whale as the very embodiment of evil, Melville conceived him as a metaphor for God, mysterious and unknowable.

That metaphor had always intrigued me. Wasn't it true, after all, that God's activity was mostly hidden from our sight, shrouded below the surface of what we can perceive, appearing only unexpectedly—like some fearsome whale or playful dolphin? As much as we try to predict His appearance or seek it out, only He knows just when, or if, He'll surface. All we can do is react.

Several years later, I would come up with a term that seemed to capture what I pondered that night in Dingle. The term was "serendestiny"—a variation of the words "serendipity" and "destiny." While serendipity refers to "the phenomenon of experiencing things not anticipated or sought for," I defined serendestiny as "the phenomenon of discovering one's destiny by responding with faith and obedience to *God-ordained* circumstances not anticipated or sought for." It was serendestiny that I had repeatedly observed in my own life over the years, and not just mine; I saw it in the lives of many others I'd known or read about, including many in Scripture.

What mattered most, I saw, is not our attempt to control or map out our destinies, but how we respond to a God who does not always bless our plans or satisfy our expectations. This, more than anything, is what determines the outcome of our lives.

Letting God write *His* story through *our* lives is often easier said than done. Many times, the circumstances He ordains—or at least sanctions—are radically different from those we would choose for ourselves. And believing that He loves us—that He is *good*—can seem nothing short of preposterous when those circumstances are not just irksome, but downright horrific.

An experience I had eight years after my visit to Ireland would prove to be a case in point.

DISCUSSION STARTERS:

❯ Are you the kind of person who likes to plan out your life, or do you take things as they come? Elaborate.

❯ How do you react when things don't go as you planned?

❯ Do you view unexpected circumstances more like the appearance of playful dolphins or fearsome whales? Explain.

2

HAITI

"Fifty million people die every year, six thousand every hour, and over one hundred every minute. But when thousands die in the same place and at the same time, we are more likely to wonder why God would allow such a thing to happen."

— Steve Farrar

IF YOU'RE ANYTHING LIKE ME, THE only unforeseen circumstances you welcome are those that are painless and clearly beneficial. A bonus in your paycheck. A surprise birthday party. A brilliant rainbow. A more precise definition of "serendipity," in fact, is "the faculty of finding valuable and *agreeable* things not sought for."[4]

---

4. Webster's New Collegiate Dictionary

When it comes to serendestiny, however, we are sometimes confronted by unforeseen circumstances that are deeply painful. The notion that God ordains, or at least sanctions, our individual and collective suffering is a subject of much controversy and debate. It is also the principal reason some believers question the goodness of God, and why many outside the faith vehemently deny His existence. A loving God, they insist, wouldn't allow bad things to happen to good people.

I am no theologian. Nor do I pretend to have "the answer" on the subject of suffering. Some unforeseen circumstances are not only painful, but hard to fathom. Yet I believe what matters most is not our ability to understand or explain dreadful events delivered via serendestiny, but our response to those events when they happen. And at no time was that truth driven home more clearly to me than a few years ago, in Haiti.

JANUARY, 2010

I arrived in Haiti on January 22, 2010, just twelve days after the horrific earthquake that killed more than 230,000 people and left 1.5 million homeless. As president of a Christian NGO[5] called Forward Edge International (FEI), I was accustomed to visiting the scenes of natural disasters. But the

---

5. NGOs (non-governmental organizations) are legally constituted agencies that operate independently from any governments. Most NGOs focus on international relief and development projects.

reports I was hearing out of Haiti were ominous, and I was glad to be traveling with Nick Rogers, a retired National Guard colonel who'd helped lay the groundwork for our recovery efforts in the Gulf Coast after Hurricane Katrina; Bob Craddock, our Director of Partnerships; and Daniel Combes, a videographer and former classmate of Bob's at Multnomah University.

At 6'4", and with a spine as straight as a flagpole, Nick looked like a colonel even in jeans and a T-shirt. A former tight end on the Oregon State football team, Nick was still haunted by the ball he'd dropped in the end zone during the 1965 Rose Bowl—a memory only partially erased when his team was inducted into OSU's Football Hall of Fame.

Balancing out Nick's machismo was Bob, an affable Canadian with brown eyes and a salt-and-pepper soul patch on his chin. Frequently the butt of Canadian jokes back at the office, Bob had a gracious way of deflecting our teasing. His laidback attitude and Dan's low key, dry sense of humor would add a much-needed dose of levity during the dark, stressful days that lay ahead.

With the Port-au-Prince airport closed to commercial traffic, we were forced to fly from Miami to the Dominican Republic (the DR) where we boarded a single-engine Cessna bound for Jacmel, a small town on Haiti's southern coast. As I watched the DR's lush, green terrain give way to the brown, deforested landscape of Haiti, I felt a familiar mix of excitement and apprehension.

On landing in Jacmel, we discovered that the airport had been commandeered by peacekeeping Canadian soldiers. Some sat behind makeshift desks in the airport's terminal, others stacked boxes of MREs (Meals Ready to Eat), still others patrolled the tarmac with loaded C7 rifles.

After waiting for more than an hour, we were met by a slender Haitian man named Gerald driving a pick-up truck with a canopy on back. We loaded our gear into Gerald's truck, then headed for downtown Jacmel. Known for its vibrant art scene, Jacmel was full of nineteenth-century town houses trimmed with cast-iron pillars and balconies imported from France; its architectural features, in fact, would later influence New Orleans. As Gerald steered his truck along Jacmel's main street, we mourned the damage to these buildings: some scarred with frightful cracks, many totally destroyed. An endless row of pup tents lined both sides of the street—each inhabited by a displaced and traumatized family.

In the aftermath of the earthquake, tens of thousands had fled the capital, Port-au-Prince, and returned in panic to their ancestral homes. Many of these refugees were now crowded into Jacmel's soccer stadium, our first stop. Little more than a muddy field ringed by a shabby wooden fence, the stadium brimmed with refugees: young mothers holding newborn babies; old men huddled in silence; restless teenagers looking for ways to conquer their boredom. At one end of the stadium, under the watchful eye of armed Canadian soldiers, scores of anxious survivors waited in line for food and water. The stench of human waste emanating from makeshift latrines was sharp and inescapable.

After Dan shot some video to brief our faithful donors and mobilize volunteers, Gerald drove us to a nearby neighborhood where he'd arranged for us to stay in his one-story, cinder-block home. Since Haitians had always been more afraid of hurricanes than earthquakes (there hadn't been an earthquake in Haiti for more than a hundred years), their favorite building materials were cinder block and concrete—a fact that directly contributed to the earthquake's astronomical death toll. Not surprisingly, the jagged cracks in Gerald's home, along with the heavy concrete ceiling in our bedroom, left us watchful and uneasy.

Directly across the road from Gerald's home was a tiny church building, also cinder block, with glassless windows and a tin roof. Dozens of survivors squatted in a makeshift campsite pitched in a field in front of the church, and Bob and I went to meet them.

Within seconds we were surrounded by a gaggle of children: girls with colorful beads braided into their hair, and boys with saucer eyes and the most perfect teeth I had ever seen. They trailed us into the church building, and after sitting on one of the church's crude wooden benches, I found myself with a child on each knee and the rest clinging to my shoulders.

Suddenly, the children began to sing. At first I thought they were singing in Creole. But as I listened more closely, I realized that they were singing, in English, a song I recognized, written by Israel Houghton. "I am not forgotten…I am not forgotten… He calls me by name."

Tears pooled in my eyes.

I believed—or at least *wanted* to believe—that God's eye was on these tiny sparrows. But I also knew that the world's media would soon move on to other stories. *God's* eye might be on them, but most other eyes—temporarily attracted by the earthquake—would eventually turn away. *What would happen to them?* I wondered.

After two days in Jacmel, Nick, Bob, Dan and I loaded our gear into a rented SUV and headed for Port-au-Prince. What we found there was the stuff of nightmares.

Our first glimpse of the horror came in Leogane, a port town of 135,000, eighteen kilometers west of Port-au-Prince and the epicenter of the earthquake. As many as 30,000 people had died here in a matter of seconds, a fact made horribly real to us by kilometer after kilometer of flattened homes, schools and church buildings. An estimated 80-90 percent of Leogane's buildings had been damaged, making it the worst-hit area in the country.

Midway through Leogane, we got out of the car to visit a children's home where one of our driver's relatives worked, and were instantly surrounded by a small mob of earthquake survivors, desperate for food and water. But we had nothing to give them. As a "Phase II" disaster-response organization, Forward Edge specialized in *long-term* recovery work, long after the first responders have left. Our mission on this trip was limited to assessing the damage, forming partnerships and determining a long-term response. Heartbroken, we got back into the SUV and continued on toward Port-au-Prince.

The devastation we found there was overwhelming. The Presidential Palace—much larger than it appeared on television—was completely destroyed, its white, twin domes resting sideways atop tons of rubble. Twenty eight of Haiti's twenty nine government buildings, including the Legislative Palace (Haiti's Parliament) and the Palace of Justice (Haiti's Supreme Court) had been razed by the earthquake, leaving a country already lacking in leadership on the brink of anarchy.

When we arrived at the Cathedrale de Port-au-Prince—Haiti's national cathedral—we found only four walls encircling a pile of rubble. Barely ten yards from the ruined cathedral, a white-haired woman knelt at the foot of a giant crucifix. "Oh, Jesus…Jesus…Jesus," the woman wailed at the top of her lungs—a cry that pierced our hearts.

Anxious to connect with local health-care providers, we made our way to *Hopital* OFATMA, a small clinic in the *Cite Militaire* sector of Port-au-Prince. After meeting with the hospital director, we visited the patients' ward, where we met a young woman whose leg had just been amputated. The pre-med student had been trapped for four days in the ruins of her collapsed school.

"My best friend's head was pinned against my chest," she told us, her cheeks wet with tears. "At the end of the second day, my friend died. We had both been praying to Jesus. But for some reason, I lived. She didn't."

I felt my heart, already overwhelmed by what I'd seen, swell even more.

"Early on the third day," the girl continued, "I heard someone yelling from outside. 'Is anyone in there?' I yelled back, 'YES!'

"'Do you have any money?'" the voice yelled back. 'No,' I said.

"It was the last I heard from him. He just left me there."

It would be forty-eight more hours before the girl was rescued, and only after rescue workers—with no other way to free her—had been forced to cut off her dead friend's head.

It was just one of thousands of heart-breaking stories the earthquake had left in its wake. And I felt ill-equipped to answer the question clearly lingering in the young girl's heart: Why had *her* prayers been answered, while her friend's had not? I was confident of only one thing: how she processed her experience and grief—and how the family of the dead girl processed theirs—would profoundly affect the ongoing story of their lives. Serendestiny had dealt them a terrible blow, and their futures hung in the balance.

Our final stop that day was a refugee camp in the Port-au-Prince suburb of Carrefour (Car-foo). It was just after nightfall when we pulled up to the camp's front gate and entered a world more like hell than any settlement on earth.

There were people everywhere—thousands of them—crammed into donated tents or makeshift shelters fashioned from tree branches and plastic tarps. Scores of charcoal fires flickered in the darkness, filling the compound with smoke and adding to its hellish appearance. As our SUV rolled slowly through the mass of refugees, some pressed their hands against its windows, gaping curiously at the *blancs*[6] inside. It was, to say the least, unnerving.

At last we came to a closed green gate, deep inside the

6. The Creole word for "white people"

compound. Our driver honked the horn and the gate opened, revealing a two-story, concrete building. For some reason, as the gate closed behind us, I thought of Davy Crockett and the Alamo.

We were greeted by a tall Haitian man, who appeared to be in his early thirties. "My name is Danny," he said in impeccable English. "Welcome to Grace Village."

From the conversation that followed we learned that Danny was the son of Bishop and Madam Jeune, respected Haitian church leaders and founders of a Christian ministry called Grace International. The twelve-acre property we had just passed through was the Grace International headquarters. It included a large, quasi-functional hospital, a church building where more than a thousand people met for weekly church services, a school building, a guesthouse for out-of-town visitors, and a home for fifty-two girls. All these buildings, Danny said—with the exception of the hospital—were either heavily damaged or completely destroyed.

"When the earthquake hit, the wall surrounding our property collapsed in several places," Danny explained. "Within hours, 20,000 people were squatting on our land."

Later that night, as we sat on the steps of the now-empty girls' home (the girls were too scared to re-enter it and were sleeping inside two large shipping containers) Danny told us his story. The youngest of four Jeune brothers, Danny had been born in Haiti but attended high school and college in the States. After college, he'd played professional basketball in France for five years before returning to help with his parents' ministry. His brothers had moved away, and when the earthquake struck, his parents were on a speaking tour in the States.

"I believe God planned for me to be here," he confided, his voice cracking with emotion. "But I can't do this on my own. I need help."

I'd seen my share of disasters—Ground Zero in Manhattan just days after 9/11; Mississippi and New Orleans after Hurricane Katrina; Nicaragua after Hurricanes Mitch and Felix; and Sri Lanka after the Indian Ocean Tsunami. But the situation in Haiti was different. As I tossed and turned in my sleeping bag that night, the children in Jacmel and the girl at *Hopital* OFATMA haunted my dreams.

The next morning, as I wolfed down an MRE breakfast, Danny approached me with an unexpected question. "The mayor of Carrefour has been meeting with survivors every day at four," he said. "Will you come to today's meeting with me?"

Exhausted and emotionally drained, there was nothing in my flesh that wanted to say "yes." But there was also no legitimate reason to say "no." *Maybe it'll make a difference*, I thought.

And so, accompanied by Danny, Nick, Bob and Dan, I arrived around 3:45 p.m. at the site of that day's meeting—a small park approximately five kilometers west of Grace Village. When we arrived, more than two hundred people had already gathered, including six distinguished-looking Haitians seated up front in a row of folding chairs. To the right of the dignitaries were several U.S. military officers—members of the Marine Expeditionary Force who were helping with the recovery effort. We were about to sit near the back when a neatly-dressed

Haitian man—seeing our white faces[7]—ushered us to the front to a row of chairs facing the Marines.

"That's Haiti's Secretary of State!" Danny whispered excitedly as we sat down. "He's the guy at the end with the glasses and white shirt. The guy in the light blue suit is the mayor."

The Secretary of State? I thought. *What's* he *doing here?*

Minutes later the meeting was called to order. Danny pulled his chair close to mine so he could translate from Creole to English. Nick was on my right, his commanding presence adding much-needed stature to our team. If I was Sherriff Woody, Nick was Buzz Lightyear.

"The floor is now open for anyone to speak," the Secretary of State announced.

A small man near the back of the crowd responded first, appealing to the dignitaries to provide more for earthquake survivors. "We need food!" he pleaded. "Our families are starving!"

Danny elbowed me in the ribs. "This is a good time to speak," he whispered, a sudden urgency in his voice. "Say something. *Say something!*"

Not wanting to disappoint him, I rose to my feet and introduced myself. "My name is Joseph Anfuso. I'm the president of a Christian NGO called Forward Edge International."

---

7. In Haiti, white foreigners are assumed to have abundant resources, a fact that gives them more "access to power" than the average citizen.

Since my sole objective was to endorse Danny, I immediately shifted the focus to Grace Village. "This is Danny Jeune," I continued, turning toward Danny. "He is responsible for a refugee camp of 20,000 people right here in Carrefour. He is a good man. His father and mother, Joel and Doris Jeune, have a ministry called Grace International; they have been serving the people of Haiti for more than thirty years." I turned toward the Secretary of State. "If there is anything you can do to get Danny more food, tarps and hygiene kits, I can assure you they will be put to good use." Not sure what else to add, I sat down.

"*Merci*," the Secretary said, his eyes fixed on mine. Then he said something else in Creole I didn't understand.

"What did he say?" I whispered to Danny.

"We'll come back to you later," Danny translated.

Come back to me? I thought. *But I have nothing else to say!*

The meeting picked up steam, and I realized that there was more anger and frustration in the crowd than I had previously understood. "We need food!" person after person pleaded. "Why don't you help us?! Our families are starving!"

More than an hour passed, with each statement more heated than the last. Finally, a tall young man in the center of the crowd jumped up and pointed angrily at the row of politicians. "You're all *thieves!*" he shouted. "Nothing but *thieves!*"

The Secretary rose to his feet. "Unless you retract that word 'thieves' I'll have you *removed* from the meeting!" he barked. The tension hung in the air for several seconds, and then the Secretary made the following pronouncement.

"We don't need more speeches. We need *solutions!*"

He then turned and looked me squarely in the face. I glanced over my shoulder to make sure he wasn't addressing someone else. But there was no one else there. Every eye in the crowd, including the row of dignitaries and the U.S. military contingent, *was locked on me.*

I'm only in Haiti because God called me here, I thought. *I'm only at this meeting because Danny invited me. I don't have* solutions *for this catastrophe. I'm only here because I responded with faith and obedience to God's call!*

Only one thing was clear to me in that moment, as I struggled to gather my thoughts. I was locked in the grip of serendestiny. God's plans were unfolding, in the midst of unimaginable suffering, through circumstances not anticipated or sought for. And not just God's plans for me, but for Forward Edge, for Danny and Grace International and, on the broadest scale, for the nation of Haiti.

How we responded—something we'll see later—would shape the course and character of our destinies.

DISCUSSION STARTERS:

❯ Can you share an experience you've had that left you questioning the goodness and sovereignty of God? Were you able to find any help in the Bible?

❯ Why do you think God allows tragic circumstances in the lives of believers and non-believers alike?

❯ Read Matthew 10:29-30. How do you think "the perfect will of God" might differ from "the permissive will of God?"

3

DELHI

. . . .

"For most of my life I struggled to find God, to know God, to love God...Now I wonder whether I have sufficiently realized that during all this time God has been trying to find me, to know me, and to love me...The question is not 'How am I to love God?' but 'How am I to let myself be loved by God?' God is looking into the distance for me, trying to find me, and longing to bring me home."

— Henri Nouwen

. . . .

As i'm sure you've noticed from your own experience, sometimes our awareness of serendestiny—of God orchestrating circumstances to reveal His plan—comes only through hindsight. It's only *after* an experience that we can connect the dots and see how events that once seemed random jell into previously unseen patterns, rich with meaning.

41

This, at least, has been the case for me.

MARCH, 2006

Five years before the 2010 Haiti earthquake, I traveled to the other side of the world to the scene of another major disaster— the Indian Ocean Tsunami—to see how Forward Edge could help. Accompanying me on that trip were my friends, Doug and Katy Crane, and another good friend and Forward Edge board president, Don Moen.

After four days in Sri Lanka, just off the southern tip of India, assessing the damage and meeting with potential partners, we all flew to India to participate in the dedication of a village for Tibetan refugees. Doug and Katy had assisted with this project, and they invited Don and me to join them.

Our first stop was the Indian capital of New Delhi, where we would stay at the New Delhi Oberai, a five-star hotel in the heart of the city. Joining us at the Oberoi was a small delegation of U.S. patrons, who—like Doug and Katy—had flown to India for the dedication. Among them were a former U.S. congressman from Washington; an oil executive from Texas; the Washington D.C. architect who'd designed the Tibetan village; and the leader of the U.S. delegation, Doug Coe.

Recently named one of America's twenty-five most influential evangelicals,[8] Coe was also known as "the stealth

---

8. TIME magazine, February 2005 issue.

Billy Graham"—a status he'd earned by traveling the world, incognito, sharing the love of Christ. A tall, swarthy man with penetrating brown eyes and a deep, authoritative voice, Doug had befriended and prayed with numerous religious leaders and heads of state over the years, including the Dalai Lama.

"How can we serve you?" one of Doug's friends had asked the Dalai Lama years earlier.

"You can build a village for Tibetan refugees," the Dalai Lama had replied.

"As followers of Jesus, we would be honored to do that," Doug's friend agreed. And they had.

The day after our arrival in New Delhi, our group was invited to the home of Charles Mendies, a Nepali-born friend of Coe's who also happened to be a friend of mine.

"Namaste!" Charles greeted us. "Come in! Come in!"

We entered his home, took off our shoes, and stepped down a narrow entryway into a large, high-ceilinged room where Casablanca fans blew cool air against the top of our heads. I took a seat in the middle of a sectional sofa, with Doug Coe and the former congressman on my right, the oil executive on my left, and the D.C. architect facing us in an overstuffed chair. Two Nepali boys dressed in traditional garb—long cotton tunics and pillbox caps—watched us from a second-floor balcony.

After a sari-clad woman served us tea, the conversation careened into a hodgepodge of reminiscences. Some in the group had arrived in India several days earlier, and Charles had arranged for them to see the sights. They'd even flown to the border of Pakistan and Afghanistan, where, protected by armored vehicles mounted with machine guns, they'd visited the Khyber Pass.

"I don't think I'll tell my wife about that part of the trip," the former congressman joked.

As one story flowed into the next, I began to feel a lump in my throat, and my heart pounded in my chest. It was a sensation I'd grown accustomed to over the years—a physiological sign that there was something I was supposed to say. But what I wanted to say was more personal, more vulnerable than the current chit chat, and I wondered if it was a good idea. *I might be better off just letting them think of me as the president of a Christian NGO*, I thought, as beads of sweat gathered on my forehead. *Why risk tarnishing my reputation?*

But what I was experiencing with these men had begun to overwhelm me. The contrast between the Spartan lifestyle of my first visit to India decades earlier and the lavish accommodations at the Oberoi, combined with the disparity between my early history and the stature of my present company, was too extreme to go unmentioned.

"There's something I need to share with you guys," I blurted at the next lull in the conversation. "It might take me a while, though. Would that be all right?"

Every eye turned in my direction.

"Sure, Joe," Doug finally said. "Go ahead. Take your time."

No turning back now, I thought.

"I was here, in Delhi, more than thirty years ago," I began. "My journey to the East actually ended just a few miles from here, on the rooftop of a flea-bag hotel. I was twenty-three years old at the time, flat broke, and at the end of my rope."

I paused for a moment to gather my thoughts. Many things had factored into my trip to India back then, many experiences and struggles that only came to make sense later. *How much should I tell them?*

"My dad was a congressman from New York," I continued, conscious of the former congressman to my left. "He rubbed shoulders with some of the world's great leaders—men like John Kennedy and Lyndon Johnson, as well as popes, movie stars and foreign heads of state.

"As a boy, I did my best to live up to my dad. I studied hard in school and got good grades. There was this unspoken expectation that I had to someday fill his shoes. And as a boy, those shoes seemed very, very big.

"I was also a twin, but my twin and I weren't identical. Frank was much bigger than me, and he had a more outgoing personality. Since twins are constantly compared, I often felt inferior to Frank—a feeling that only intensified when we became teenagers and girls entered the picture.

"Frank and I were sent off to Catholic boarding school when we were eleven. We spent the seventh through twelfth grades in these schools, and even though we heard a lot about God and Christianity, we never came to know Christ. By the time we graduated high school, we'd both pretty much lost interest in the Christian faith.

"Then, in the middle of my freshman year of college, my dad died suddenly of a heart attack. I was seventeen years old. It would take too long to explain how my father's death affected me, but more than anything I felt as if a golden anvil had been lifted from my shoulders—as if all the pressures and expectations of my childhood had suddenly vanished—and it wasn't long before I started questioning everything."

I paused for a moment to gauge how the others were reacting to my story. They seemed interested, so I pressed on.

"A major turning point came in the middle of my senior year of college. It was 1969, and I was an exchange student in London. Up until then I'd been on a kind of conveyer belt to law school. My dad was a lawyer, my older brother was a lawyer, and as far back as I could remember, *I* was going to be a lawyer. I took the LSATs and did well. But when it came time to send in my applications, I decided against it. I didn't know what I wanted to do with my life at that point, and after traveling around Europe, my only ambition was to see more of the world.

"I spent the next three years doing just that. I rode a motorcycle across Europe, traveled with Frank and several friends to California and Hawaii, and worked on a ship in the Pacific. I found myself on a hippie commune in Northern California near the coastal town of Mendocino, where a series of unforeseen and, frankly, unwanted circumstances began to interrupt my journey.

"First, I discovered that Frank, my twin, had become a follower of Christ—what we called at the time a Jesus Freak—and was living on a Christian commune not far from me. This came as a total shock, and not something I thought of as good. I was deeply entrenched in the idea that there were many ways to God and that all roads led to the same place. How could Jesus be the *only* way? So after three days visiting with Frank and hearing all about Jesus, I left him and set out again to find my own spiritual path—one that would be just as good if not better than Frank's.

"But the interruptions kept happening. Just a couple months later, while returning from a hippie gathering in Colorado, the school bus I was traveling in got pulled over by a pastor I'd met at Frank's commune. He thought our bus belonged to one of the Christian communes that were springing up in California at the time. *This is crazy*, I remember thinking. *What were the odds of bumping into Frank's pastor?!*

"A few weeks later, I decided to continue my spiritual search by traveling to India. But the night before heading East, the commune I was living on was visited by the leader of a neighboring commune, a German woman named Sabine Ball. To everyone's surprise, Sabine had recently surrendered her life to Christ, and couldn't wait to tell us about it. We were not very interested in what she had to say.

"The next morning, I left for India. I hitched across the U.S. to Massachusetts, where I picked apples to earn enough money to buy a one-way plane ticket to Germany. From Germany, I traveled by train to Istanbul, where I booked passage on a freighter heading east across the Black Sea. From eastern Turkey I took public buses across Iran and Afghanistan, then hitched a ride in a VW van through the Khyber Pass to the border of Pakistan and India.

"And then it happened again. While waiting to pass through Indian customs, a group of western Jesus Freaks appeared out of nowhere, handing out tracts. I couldn't believe it. *What did I have to do to get away from these people?*

"I ended up spending the next year and a half in India and Nepal, collecting exotic experiences and continuing my search for spiritual answers in the East. I visited the birthplace of Buddhism, spent a month at a Tibetan Buddhist monastery, and trekked to the base camp of Mount Everest.

"Finally, I ended up here—in Delhi—trying to extend my Indian visa so I could stay longer. By then I was about broke and could barely afford a tiny room on the rooftop of a grungy hotel. On the day before my visa appointment, I was sitting on the cot in my hotel room, meditating. At first, I could hear the sound of rickshaw bells, taxi horns and Indian music on the street below. Gradually, the street noise faded, and all I could hear was the beating of my heart. With my eyes closed, I focused on my breath.

"Then, for no apparent reason, I opened my eyes and watched in wonder as the top horizontal and mid-vertical boards of my hotel room door became illuminated in the form of a cross. I had a single, simple thought: *It's Jesus. Jesus is the way.* And then the cross faded, and I was back in India again, the taxi horns and rickshaw bells even louder than they'd been before."

I paused to see if the others in the room were still tracking with me. Their affirming smiles assured me they were, so I proceeded.

"The next day, my request for a new Indian visa was denied, and within forty-eight hours—and with the help of a one-way plane ticket from my brother, Vic—I was flying back to the

States. When I arrived in New York, I found that my entire family—my mom, my brother Vic, my two older sisters, and two out of three of their spouses—had all become followers of Christ while I was away. Two months later—after weeks of studying the Bible and spending time with my family and other Christians I'd met in New York—I, too, became a follower of Jesus. That was thirty-one years ago, and I've been following Him ever since."

Silence filled the room, and I wondered how my distinguished companions would respond to my far-out story. Had it diminished their opinions of me?

Doug Coe had been leaning back in his chair with his eyes closed the whole time I'd been talking. Now, he reached out and pressed my hand.

"On a scale of one to ten, that was a ten, Joe," he said softly. "The Hound of Heaven nips at all our heels. And you were fortunate to let Him run you down."

I felt a warm and benevolent presence in the room, as if Doug's blessing was the echo of a much greater benediction: the blessing of my heavenly Father.

The next day, I flew with my companions to the Indian hill station of Mussoorie for the dedication of the Tibetan village. It was beautiful, and meeting the Dalai Lama was a treat. But my experience in Charles Mendies' home would have a deeper, more enduring impact.

As I looked back at where I'd been, and where God had brought me, it became more clear to me than ever that my Christian conversion had been preceded by a series of divinely-orchestrated events not anticipated or sought for: the conversion of my twin brother; my roadside encounter with Frank's pastor; the visit by Sabine to my Mendocino commune; the Jesus Freaks at the Pakistani/Indian border; and my vision of a cross in Old Delhi. It was not *my* seeking that led me to Christ. It was the seeking of a God who loved me, reached out to me, and longed to bring me home.

"No man can come to Me unless the Father draws him," Jesus said. That's why so many of us once estranged from God, then reconciled, have stories of circumstances unforeseen and interruptions unwanted—stories of serendestiny.

We may not think of it as such at the time. But when we recognize God's activity in our lives—activity that has nothing to do with our own thinking or agendas—we begin to acknowledge, perhaps reluctantly, that Someone greater than ourselves is trying to shape our destinies. And it's our response to that Someone that invariably determines the ultimate story of our lives.

DISCUSSION STARTERS:

❱ If you're a follower of Christ, were there any unforeseen circumstances or experiences that led to you becoming a Christ follower? If so, what were they?

❱ When these circumstances or experiences first confronted you, did you think it might be God intervening in your life? If not, how did you interpret them?

JOSEPH ANFUSO

4

SURRENDER

....

"I gave in, and admitted that God was God."

— C.S. Lewis

....

SERENDESTINY HAS LONG PLAYED A ROLE in the unfolding of god's plans for people's lives. The Bible is replete with examples: Moses' encounter with the burning bush;[9] Joseph languishing in prison before he was asked to interpret Pharaoh's dream;[10] Mary's visit with the Angel Gabriel;[11] Saul's vision on the road to Damascus.[12] Our own serendestiny moments may be less dramatic, but they are no less real, and no less central to the

---

9. Exodus 3

10. Genesis 41:1-7

11. Luke 1:26-38

12. Acts 9:1-9

unfolding of God's plans for us.

It's one thing to *experience* God's interventions, though, and another to respond with faith and obedience. We always have the option to choose disbelief or defiance, as Jonah did. Total surrender is a voluntary but critical step in our journey with Christ—a step that often confronts us through the phenomenon of serendestiny.

If we are going to discover and pursue the best story of our lives, our following must be radical and without conditions. We must *accept* God's invitation to follow Him, even when we don't know where He's leading or what the outcome will be.

NOVEMBER, 1973

After returning to New York from India in the fall of 1973, the discovery of my family's conversion was another in the series of serendestiny moments that eventually pointed me toward Christ.

Since I had no money and no clear plans for the future, I accepted my brother Vic's invitation to live with him and his wife, Kathy, in their Tudor-style home on the north shore of Long Island. My room was their newly-renovated attic.

"Hey Joe, I got a phone call last night from someone you knew in California," Vic informed me after I'd been living with him for a couple of weeks. "Do you remember a woman named Sabine Ball? She's living in Brooklyn now."

Of course I remembered Sabine. She was the German

woman who'd shared her Christian testimony at the Mendocino commune where I lived just before leaving for India.

At Vic's urging, I decided to pay Sabine a visit. She was living with several other Christ followers in a brownstone they called The Shepherd's House near Fort Greene Park. We sat on a sofa in the brownstone's living room.

"So what have you been up to lately, Joseph?" she asked. A strikingly-beautiful woman in her mid-forties with blue eyes and a strong German accent, Sabine had the air of a Prussian princess and always called me Joseph, not Joe.

I told her I'd just returned from Asia a couple of weeks ago, and that I'd spent the better part of two years in India and Nepal.

"Really? I was in Nepal back in 1968. I spent three months there, two in a Tibetan Buddhist monastery."

"Really? Which monastery?"

"It was just outside Bodhnath, a place called Kopan. Do you know it?"

I could hardly believe my ears. That was the same monastery *I* had visited three years later. *I know exactly where you're coming from*, Sabine's eyes seemed to assure me as our conversation rambled on. And the fact that she had traveled a similar path to my own, and now was a Christian, made me uncomfortable.

When I stood up to leave, Sabine walked me to the door.

"Joseph, why don't you ask *God* to show you if He's real?" she said, just before we parted. "He can do that, you know. He knows everything about you, and He wants to reveal Himself to you. Why don't you ask *Him*?"

A week later, I was sitting cross-legged on my bed in Vic and Kathy's attic. It was nearly midnight, and the room was pitch black. I'd been trying to meditate for more than an hour, slowly shifting my attention from my breath to my head, my neck, my shoulders, my chest.

Why don't you ask Him? Sabine's question reverberated in my head. I'd been reading a Bible Vic had given me, expecting to align it comfortably with my own ideas about God and spirituality. But the more I'd read—particularly in the New Testament—the more clear and unique its message appeared. It wasn't long, in fact, before I found myself faced with a troubling decision: was the Bible's message true or just a foolish fabrication?

With some reluctance, I rose from my bed and stepped toward the center of the room. *This is crazy,* I thought as I lowered myself to my knees. *Am I really supposed to believe there's a God up there listening to me?*

"If you're there," I prayed, nearly smiling at the absurdity of it all, "show me if you're real. I want to know. *Show me* if you're real."

Three nights later, I had a dream. I was in Bodhgaya, the small town in India where Buddha had allegedly achieved enlightenment. I'd visited there twice during my travels. All around me, men in turbans and women in saris were running through the streets, shouting and waving their arms frantically above their heads. As I wandered through the chaos, I seemed to be invisible, yet fully present.

Where's the stupa? I wondered, thinking of the great stone obelisk that marked the spot where Buddha had been sitting when he became "The Enlightened One." And then I saw it—or what remained of it. The monument was nothing but a pile of rubble, barely one stone atop another.

As I stood there, the sky became dark and foreboding. Desperate to find shelter, I ducked inside a nearby hovel. As soon as I entered I was confronted by a creature of some kind, its horns and hooves reminiscent of a goat, but much more menacing. It was trying to hurt me, to kill me, to force me under.

And then I woke up.

What was that *about?* I tried to slow my panicked breathing as I pulled back my sheets and switched on the lamp. My first instinct was to dismiss the dream as a food-induced nightmare. But it was too vivid and seemed too purposeful. Though my interpretation repelled me, I could not help but grasp the dream's meaning.

It was a warning about my spiritual quest, my years of searching for a "path" I could call my own. The *stupa*—reaching heavenward like an outstretched arm—symbolized man's efforts to find or become one with God by means of his own understanding and strength. Its destruction—along with the presence of an evil creature—conveyed the futility of this pursuit.

Could this strange and frightening dream be a direct, unwelcome answer to my Sabine-inspired prayer?

Two days later, I paid another visit to The Shepherd's House. The dream had fueled my interest in Christianity, and I was willing—if not eager—to look more closely at the claims of Christ.

When I arrived, I found twenty or thirty people gathered in the living room for what appeared to be an informal church service. A small man with a scraggily red beard and Scottish brogue was addressing the group from a chair on the far side of the room. Not wanting to draw attention to myself, I sat on the floor near the door in front of a large, balding man with anchors tattooed on his forearms.

As soon as the Scotsman was done preaching and the group started to break up, I crossed the room to confront him.

"Why do you Christians believe Jesus is the *only* way?" I challenged him, probably with a hint of condescension in my voice. "Can't you just follow His teachings without insisting every other approach to God is inferior, even false?"

The Scotsman accepted the challenge, and for the next few minutes we engaged in an intellectual debate. We'd been at it for a while when I noticed that the tattooed man I'd been sitting in front of was watching us from a nearby sofa. He was clearly eavesdropping, and as soon as my conversation with the Scotsman ended I excused myself and walked over to introduce myself.

"My name's Joseph," I said warily, certain that the big man's views were not in line with mine.

"Robert," the big man grinned. I was suddenly aware of my contrived-looking getup: my wool Tibetan jacket with the stand-up collar, my turquoise and corral earring and my handmade moccasins.

"Ya know, dare's sumptin' I been wantin' ta ayx you," the big man said in a thick Brooklyn accent.

"Oh? What's that?" I was fairly sure I didn't want to know.

"Why don't ya just get auf yur trip?" the big man then barked, his eyes scanning me from head to toe.

I reeled back, a bit dazed. No one had ever talked to me like that before. But I knew in that moment that there was nothing about my carefully crafted persona—my colorful outfit, spiritual insights or fanciful adventures—that would impress this simple, honest man who now confronted me. I felt naked in his presence.

"Ah...well...I'm not sure I know what you mean," I stammered, fumbling for something to say. But there was nothing to say. The man had made his point, and I was speechless.

Shaken, I fled into the nearby kitchen to see what time it was. Ten thirty. I groaned. The last train from Penn Station to Vic's home on Long Island left at 10:45. There was no way I'd make it.

Begrudgingly, I asked the Scotsman if I could spend the night.

Five hours later I was lying awake on a bunk bed in The Shepherd's House "brothers dorm." The others in the room were asleep, and, fearful of waking them, I waited for the wail of a passing siren to muffle the sound of my shifting under the sheets.

Staring into the darkness, I found myself battling the big man's challenge: *Why don't you just get off your trip?*

Like lava in a volcano, three words began to force their way upward toward my throat. I give up…I give up…*I give up!*

I wanted to shout these words into the brothers dorm, but when I pictured myself surrounded by the swarm of Bible-thumping evangelists who would no doubt descend on my conversion-ready self, I was jolted back to my senses. The eruption in my heart subsided. But it was just a matter of time, I suspected, before the persona I had fashioned would fail even my own reality test.

Four days later, on March 23, 1974, I surrendered my life to Jesus at my sister Maria's home on Long Island. A series of serendestiny moments—my vision of the cross in Delhi, my family's conversion, my re-encounter with Sabine, my dream of Bodhgaya and the challenge of the big man at The Shepherd's House—all contributed to my surrender. But I had no idea at the time that "surrender" was not just the starting point of my journey with Christ; it was a place I would have to repeatedly re-visit if I wanted to reach the journey's end.

And just as serendestiny had helped draw me into a relationship with Christ, it would also be a primary means by which that relationship would deepen.

DISCUSSION STARTERS:

❱ When you first surrendered your life to Christ, were you aware of the cost you'd have to pay in terms of your lifestyle and priorities? If not, when and how did this cost first become apparent to you?

❱ Read Romans 12:1-2. What do you think it means to "offer your [bodies] as a living sacrifice to God?"

JOSEPH ANFUSO

5

GOD'S LOVE

"We should be astonished at the goodness of God, stunned that He should bother to call us by name, our mouths wide open at His love..."

— Brennan Manning

I AM CONVINCED THAT THERE IS no more important factor in the process of growing and enduring as a follower of Christ than a deep, personal *experience* of God's love. It's not surprising, then, that Paul the Apostle would "kneel before the Father" and pray that those already converted would be *"rooted and grounded* in love," able to "grasp how wide and long and high and deep is the love of Christ, and to *know* this love that surpasses knowledge."[13] For whether we like it or not, God permits

13. Ephesians 3:13-21, italics added

mighty winds to buffet the lives of those who follow Him, and only those "rooted and grounded in love" can keep from blowing over.

As we've seen, God often reveals His love for us through circumstances that we neither anticipate nor seek. It's our response to these circumstances that determines whether or not His love takes root in our hearts, and whether or not we discover and embrace the destiny He has planned for us.

This was certainly true for me.

NOVEMBER, 1974

I do not consider my conversion dramatic. There were no lightning bolts, no neon signs, no undeniable voices speaking to me from heaven. I simply waved the white flag and asked Jesus to take charge of my life. God had chased me, I see now, but as a new believer, I had no real *experience of His love*.

Soon after my conversion, I moved from Vic's to a Brooklyn brownstone affiliated with The Shepherd's House. It was called The Oxford Street House, or Oxford Street for short. I'd been living there for only a few days, when one of the Oxford Street "elders" approached me.

"We have a small library of cassette teaching tapes that we need someone to manage, Joe," he said. "Would you be willing to do that?"

A cassette-tape librarian? I thought. No way.

"I'd rather not," I replied, sure that God had something

grander in mind for me.

The elder saw right through me. "You know, God's going to do something wonderful in your life, Joe," he said, with more compassion than I probably deserved. "He's going to cause you to think less and less about what's in it for you, and more and more about what you can do to bless others."

Convicted and not wanting to appear prideful, I reluctantly agreed. But I was ill prepared for the long, transformational journey I had only just begun.

As months passed, I was surprised to find that my commitment to Christ—or at least my commitment to living with thirty people in a Brooklyn brownstone—was starting to waver. Unable to find work elsewhere, I'd taken a job as a "rough carpenter" at a nearby Brooklyn shipyard. I worked long, grueling days repairing the shipyard's dry docks—a physically demanding job that required chain saws, oversized drills and ten-pound sledge hammers. To add insult to injury, I was expected, like all the other residents at Oxford Street, to hand over my monthly paychecks—one of the many requirements of communal living.

Finally, after nine months at Oxford Street and eight months at the shipyard, I reached my breaking point. It had been a hard day at work, and I returned to Oxford Street weary, frustrated and confused. Without speaking to anyone, I climbed the three flights of stairs that led to the prayer room—a square, high-ceilinged room furnished only with oversized pillows. I closed the door behind me and started to cry.

"I can't live like this anymore, God!" I wept. "I can't! I can't!

I can't!"

Suddenly, I felt an unexpected presence enter the room. *Is that You, Lord?*

I felt a gentle pressure on my back, as if a heavy blanket had been draped across my shoulders. "I love you, Joseph," I heard someone say—not audibly, but deep inside my heart. "I love you…I love you…*I love you….*"

My tears flowed freely. And while the pain and confusion in my heart persisted, I was also comforted by what appeared to be the presence of God.

"And My will for your life," the inaudible voice continued, "is that you be a servant."

A servant? Don't you know who I am, God? I'm the son of a congressman! A graduate of Rutgers College! A world-traveling seeker of truth! There must be some mistake!

Then, as if the previous message was not challenging enough, the inaudible voice spoke again. "And this will *always* be My will for you, Joseph. And I love you…I love you…*I love you….*"

The pressure lifted from my shoulders and I was alone again, tearful and undone, on the floor of the empty prayer room.

Sitting up, I was flooded with conflicting emotions. On the one hand, I was intimidated. A servant? *For the rest of my life?* It was a fate too daunting, too undesirable, too seemingly impossible for me to comprehend.

But more powerful than that was a new and unprecedented knowledge that seemed to permeate my entire being. It was as if a tiny sponge, deep inside my soul, had been moistened for the very first time. I now knew, in a way I had never known before, that the God of the Bible—the living personal Creator of the universe—not only existed, but He loved me. Loved *ME*!

And so, nine full months after my conversion, I experienced for the first time the *reality* of God's love. More than a concept or something to be accepted by faith, it was now *real* to me, like a tree in my backyard or the hair on the top of my head.

Once again, it was serendestiny—God intervening in ways I'd not anticipated—that introduced me to a deeper knowledge of His reality. And, as is true for every Christ follower, it was serendestiny that would beckon me deeper still.

DISCUSSION STARTERS:

❭ Did you have a dramatic conversion experience? If not, how do you think this could have affected your subsequent walk with Christ? Explain.

❭ When and how did God first make His love real to you? Please be specific.

JOSEPH ANFUSO

6

INTO THE LIGHT

"We shy away from introspection because, however fearful the surface seems, we fear the depths still more. And we are right. There is much to fear there. If there is terror about darkness because we cannot see, there is also terror about light because we can see."

— Frederich Buechner

"Nobody escapes being wounded. We all are wounded people, whether physically, emotionally, mentally or spiritually. The main question is not 'How can we hide our wounds?' so we don't have to be embarrassed, but 'How can we put our woundedness in service of others?' When our wounds cease to be a source of shame, and become a source of healing, we have become wounded healers."

— Henri Nouwen

HAVE YOU EVER WONDERED WHY SOME followers of Christ seem to have more power and authenticity in their Christian witness than others? More than a statement of what they believe, their professions of faith seem to emanate from deep, personal experiences that have profoundly altered their lives. Their testimonies are not unlike John's description of the early disciples' experience: "that which we have heard, which we have seen with our eyes, which we have looked at and which our hands have touched."[14]

I believe one of the most important factors that determines the strength and authenticity of our Christian witness is the degree to which we're willing to invite God into the secret, wounded corners of our hearts. God already knows about these corners, of course. But He will never make Himself at home there uninvited.

The nineteenth-century theologian and author, Soren Kierkegaard, had this to say on the subject: "In every man there is something which to a certain degree prevents him from becoming perfectly transparent to himself; and this may be the case to so high a degree, and may be so inexplicably woven into relationships of life which extend far beyond himself that he almost cannot reveal himself. But he who cannot reveal himself cannot love, and he who cannot love is the most unhappy man of all."

Not surprisingly, it is often serendestiny that bids us to bare our souls. And only by accepting these invitations can we find healing and embrace the best story of our lives.

---

14. 1 John 1

OCTOBER, 1985

The first home Karen and I purchased was a small, Tudor-style Craftsman in Eureka, California. White with brown trim, it featured a brick fireplace framed by built-in bookcases, hand-cranked, European-style windows and a cozy kitchen nook overlooking a small but tidy backyard. We loved it.

We were so excited about our new home, in fact, that we didn't think to check the water pressure until after we'd moved in.

"Oh, no," I groaned as I watched a thin bead of water trickle from the spout at the kitchen sink. "I bet the plumbing in the whole house is shot!"

Panicked and feeling ripped off, I called the City Water Department.

"I doubt it's as bad as you think," a man at the other end of the line tried to comfort me. "Sometimes the pipes leading into those older homes get rusted through. We'll send over a crew to check it out."

In less than an hour (Eureka's a small town) three men in coveralls and hard hats showed up at our door and started jack hammering the pavement in front of our new home. Neighbors we hadn't met yet peered curiously from their windows.

Three hours later, one of the workers—the foreman, I presumed—rang our front doorbell. "We just turned the water back on," he said, wiping dust and sweat from his forehead.

"Why don't you check the pressure now?"

I returned to the kitchen and turned on the faucet. The same bead of water appeared.

I retraced my steps to the front door and delivered the bad news. "The pressure in the sink is no different," I told the foreman. "Which is weird, because the pressure in the bathroom is *fine*."

The foreman frowned. Brushing me aside, he went to the kitchen, unscrewed the tip of the faucet, and peered inside. He then placed the faucet head under my nose. There, nestled at its base, was a tiny pebble that had been blocking the water.

I could feel my cheeks turning red.

"Don't worry about it," the good-natured foreman said. "We get paid by the hour."

I didn't realize it then, but the pebble was a kind of prophetic object lesson—a whimsical foreshadowing of a serendestiny moment just a few months down the road.

In the eight years since Karen and I'd moved to California, I had tried to focus my heart on fulfilling God's call on my life to serve. Eureka—near the headquarters of the international church-planting ministry we'd joined, Gospel Outreach (GO)— was not lacking in opportunities. Soon after our arrival, Karen and I started a weekly home group for twenty-somethings. I also wrote articles for a local church-run newspaper and helped ghostwrite books for the founder of Gospel Outreach, Jim Durkin. In 1980, three years after moving to Eureka, I was ordained as an elder, and two years after that, a teacher. By the time Karen and I moved into our Craftsman, I had co-authored two books, edited two teaching curricula, and launched Forward Edge. I was a seemingly healthy and productive member of the Body of Christ.

Then serendestiny came knocking on my door in the form of a Gospel Outreach missionary named Jim DeGolyer. An unassuming man with thick wire-rim glasses and a full beard, Jim had come to Eureka from Ecuador to conduct a two-day seminar on the gifts of the Holy Spirit. Curious to see if Ecuador might be a good destination for Forward Edge mission teams, I invited Jim to our home for dinner.

When we finished eating, Jim, Karen and I retired to our living room. We'd been chatting for about an hour when Jim asked a strange, seemingly out-of-place question.

"Can I pray for you, Joseph?"

Pray for me? I thought. *Why would he want to do that?*

"Sure, why not?" I replied cautiously. Karen nodded her approval.

For several minutes, we stood in silence as Jim rested his hands gently against my chest.

"Thank you for my brother, Joseph," he finally said out loud. "Thank you for his tender heart and many gifts."

Another minute or two passed.

"Joseph, I'm getting a mental picture of two babies in a mother's womb. Does that mean anything to you?"

I was startled. I was a twin, of course, but how did Jim know that? Frank—who now went by Francis—had gained a reputation in recent years as a gifted evangelist and spent much of his time traveling around the country conducting seminars. Although we lived hundreds of miles apart, Francis' growing "celebrity" fed my old feelings of inferiority—feelings I'd been careful to keep secret. *Had Jim somehow heard about Francis?*

"Well, I do have a twin," I said.

A smile curled across Jim's face, and his eyes—now open—seemed to blanket me with compassion. "Thank You, Jesus," he prayed, before closing his eyes again.

Several seconds passed.

"I see a hand holding a knife," Jim said. "The hand is reaching toward a cord in the mother's womb—not an umbilical cord, but a cord connecting the two babies. The hand is placing the knife against the cord and cutting it. The babies are free now to live out their own destinies, to tell their own stories, to fulfill God's unique plans and purposes for their lives."

How did he know this? I resisted. *Someone must have told him about Francis.*

"God is showing me that for many years you've believed a lie about yourself, Joseph," Jim went on. "The lie is that you are second rate. And so, in the name of Jesus, I break the power of that lie over your life now, and forever more."

There was a moment of silence, and then Jim asked what I was feeling.

"I'm not sure," I said, trying to mask my cynicism. "I appreciate you praying for me, though. And I'll definitely take what happened here tonight to God in prayer."

The next evening Karen and I attended the first session of Jim's seminar. As a church elder, I usually sat up front, but that evening I asked Karen if we could sit near the back. Distracted by the previous night's happenings, I struggled to concentrate on Jim's message.

Why did he have to embarrass me like that? I fumed. *Aren't I free enough? I'm an elder, for God's sake, an ordained minister, a writer of books!*

But another voice, deep inside, offered a different opinion. *You know you're not free, Joseph. Why don't you just admit it? Aren't you tired of hiding the truth?*

At last, Jim was finished preaching. "Would anyone like to come forward for prayer?" he asked.

I was now in the middle of a serendestiny moment. As far back as I could remember, I had kept my deepest fears and insecurities private, especially my feelings of inferiority in comparison to Frank. And while I'd been reluctant to receive Jim's prophecy, I was now overcome with feelings of disgust. Yes, I'd received enough grace and truth over the years to function as a follower of Christ. But was I truly FREE?!

Faced with circumstances I had neither anticipated nor sought, I was now confronted with a choice: Would I spurn the opportunity this moment offered, or respond with faith and obedience? It was a choice only I could make.

I rose from my seat and made my way to the front of the church. *I don't care what people think,* I resolved.

Within just a few seconds, I was surrounded by well-meaning friends. I was vaguely aware that they were praying for me, and that their prayers were heartfelt and biblically correct. But I felt no connection to their prayers. I felt only God's presence as words only I could hear engulfed me like a tidal wave.

I love you, Joseph...I love you...I love you...I love you....

From that day forward, I experienced a new spiritual freedom in my life. Like the pebble in my faucet, a pernicious lie had been choking the flow of living water through my heart, and serendestiny had provided an opportunity for God to remove it.

The experience was so profound that to this day I pray that all God's people would know the reality of this verse from the book of Ephesians: "…everything exposed by the light becomes visible, for it is light that makes everything visible. This is why it is said: 'Wake up, O sleeper, rise from the dead and Christ will shine on you.'"[15]

DISCUSSION STARTERS:

❭ Think of two or three past experiences or current struggles that you'd be embarrassed to share with others. Now read James 5:16. What benefits do you think you and others might derive if you were more open about these things?

❭ Read John 7:38. Are you aware of any "pebbles" in your life— unforgiveness, resentment, self pity, secret sins, etc.—that might be obstructing the flow of God's life in and through you? If you are, are you willing to expose them to God's light, allowing Him to start or continue the process of removing them? (This may be a discussion you need to have with God alone or with someone you trust and respect.)

---

15. Ephesians 5:13

7

LIVING SACRIFICES

"Imagine that Jesus is calling you today. He extends a new invitation to accept His Father's love. And maybe you answer, 'Oh I know that. It's old hat.' And God answers, 'No that's what you don't know. You don't know how much I love you. The moment you think you understand is the moment you do not."

— Brennan Manning

IF YOU'VE BEEN A FOLLOWER OF Christ for any length of time, you've no doubt heard a thing or two about surrender. "Oh yes, I surrendered my life to Jesus *years* ago," you might truthfully insist. You may have even had subsequent experiences when you surrendered more fully to Christ, when you sincerely offered yourself to Him as "a living sacrifice."[16]

The problem, though, is that *living* sacrifices can crawl off the altar. Gradually, without even realizing it, we can find ourselves so absorbed in "living the Christian life" that we no longer see a need to stay connected to its Source. And even if we *do* stay connected, unforeseen circumstances invariably confront us—circumstances that require a new and fresh surrender. For it's only by responding with faith and obedience to God-ordained circumstances beyond our control that we can fully discover and embrace His best story for our lives.

SEPTEMBER, 1989

Three years after my "pebble experience," Karen and I moved from Eureka to Vancouver, Washington, just across the Columbia River from Portland.

Forward Edge was six years old by then and still legally connected to its parent ministry, Gospel Outreach (GO). Over the years, God had blessed Forward Edge, steadily increasing the number of mission teams, as well as our staff and support base. But along with growth came mounting concerns about our affiliation with GO. Forward Edge was partnering with a broad cross-section of churches: from Baptist to Presbyterian, Foursquare to non-denominational. As time passed, an increasingly smaller percentage of volunteers came from

---

16. Romans 12:1-2

churches affiliated with GO. With a vision focused on extending God's kingdom, Forward Edge no longer seemed to fit within the parameters of a single denomination.

But disconnecting would not be easy. I worried about worst-case scenarios. *What if the GO leaders wanted to hang on to Forward Edge? They had every legal right to do so. And if they did, what would become of my salary? My home? My reputation? The ministry I'd worked so hard to nurture and grow?*

For nearly three years, I'd been lifting up this challenge to God in prayer. I sought His will in Scripture; met with friends whose counsel I trusted; and tried my best to weigh the reasons for my growing discontent. I battled confusion, double-mindedness and, perhaps more than anything, fear.

It was during this season of soul searching that I heard about a conference in Kansas City. The host church was reputed to be a place where God "showed up" in unique and powerful ways. Intrigued and desperate for divine direction, I decided to attend.

I spent the week prior to the conference rafting on the Rogue River with several friends. The trip was exhilarating and unexpectedly exhausting. I arrived home, the night before my departure for Kansas City, at 1:00 in the morning. My flight was at 6:45.

Sometime between 1:30 a.m. and 5:00 a.m., I had a dream. In the dream, I was standing in a house that felt like home. On the first floor of the house, a number of interesting objects were displayed, including a large trophy and pictures of well-known people in silver frames. On the second floor of the house, I found an empty space with bare walls and not a stick of furniture.

Peering through a nearby window, I saw two painters standing on a scaffold, rolling white paint on the exterior of the house. Their faces were expressionless, and I had the sense that they took no pleasure in their work. One of the painters set down his roller, climbed through the window, and came toward me. He appeared to be asking me a question. I mumbled something in response, and he became very excited. *"That's it! That's it!"* he screamed, falling to the floor on his back and twirling around, break-dance style. He then left through the same window he'd entered, but did not return to the scaffold.

The dream jumped, and I found myself on the top floor of the house. Three young children were sitting in a circle playing some kind of game. They were laughing and having fun, and while there were no adults in the room, I had the overwhelming sense that they were safe, that everything was just as it should be.

I then stood at the threshold of a dimly-lit chamber. Smoke or incense filled the room, and I could barely make out a dancing woman twirling a long silk scarf above her head. I had an almost irresistible urge to enter the chamber, to join the woman in her dance, to let down my defenses and embrace her.

And then I woke up. *What was* that *about?*

I squinted at my alarm clock: 5:15 a.m. *My flight was leaving in ninety minutes!* I jumped out of bed, threw some clothes into a suitcase and headed for the Portland airport. Five hours later, I was landing in Kansas City, my dream almost forgotten.

The conference was at the Kansas City Convention Center,

and when I arrived more than three thousand people were already assembled in its main auditorium. A gifted worship band was playing an anointed version of *I Surrender All*. I felt an extraordinary, almost overwhelming sense of God's presence.

I found a seat near the back of the auditorium and fell to my knees. "I want Your will, God," I cried, burdened by the challenge I faced with Gospel Outreach. "Just Your will…Your will….Your will…"

As soon as the worship was over, a tall, bespectacled man strode to the podium.

"My message to you today will be on worship," he said.

Using as his text the twelfth chapter of the Book of Romans, he proceeded to expound on what he called "the true meaning of worship." It was a message I had not only heard before, but expounded on myself a time or two.

"Worship is not music," he declared. "It's not singing or dancing or clapping our hands. Worship is offering ourselves as living sacrifices to God. *This* is our reasonable service, the Bible says. This—and only this—will keep us in God's good, pleasing, and perfect will."

A wave of emotion swept over me. It was as if I was hearing the message of Romans 12 for the very first time. Yes, I'd surrendered my life to Christ—more than once, in fact. But I was now faced with a new and unique set of circumstances. If I tried to separate Forward Edge from GO, I risked losing almost everything I held most dear.

Was the price tag more than I was willing to pay?

A picture began to form in my mind. I saw myself walking

to the foot of a giant cross, bending down, and placing everything I was most afraid of losing at the foot of the cross: my salary, my reputation, my cherished and carefully-cultivated ministry. I then stood up, turned around, and walked away. I did not look back. And instantly, I felt an indescribable freedom, as if a boulder had been lifted from my shoulders.

My decision to surrender afresh to God was accompanied by a decision to move forward with trying to separate Forward Edge from Gospel Outreach. I had no idea what would come of this decision. But with peace now anchored in my heart, I knew I had nothing to fear.

That night in my hotel room, I took the shower I'd been unable to take earlier in the day. And there, under the water, I received an interpretation of my dream the night before.

The house was my life. The first floor, with its trophy and pictures of well-known people, symbolized not only the pressures I'd felt as a child to live up to my dad, but the longing throughout my life to achieve some form of worldly or spiritual success—to become "somebody" through my own wisdom and strength.

The second floor, with its painters covering the empty house in white, represented my attempts *as a Christian* to appear good and righteous. I thought of what Jesus told the Pharisees: "You're like whitewashed tombs which appear beautiful on the outside, but inside are full of dead men's bones and all uncleanness."[17]

The top floor was a picture of what *God* wanted for my life:

---

17. Matthew 23:27

childlike trust and intimacy with Him. I believe the dancing woman was a representation of the Holy Spirit, wooing me toward a relationship of deeper intimacy. It wasn't pseudo-spirituality or good deeds that God desired; it was *a relationship*. Was this the answer I had given the joyless painter—the answer that made him twirl playfully on his back?

Tears commingled with the shower water on my face as I sobbed. *I love you, Joseph*, a now-familiar voice echoed inside my heart. *I love you...I love you...I love you.*

By now, almost fifteen years after my first surrender to Christ, I was starting to realize that recognizing God's plan for my life might have less to do with studying the Bible or knowing my spiritual gifts, than with embracing the story He was scripting for me—a story that unfolded through circumstances I did not anticipate or seek.

DISCUSSION STARTERS:

❯ What things in your life are you most afraid of losing?

❯ What do you think would keep you from bringing these things to the foot of the cross, then turning around and walking away?

The tower overlooking Dingle Harbor on the west coast of Ireland.

Karen and me in the backyard of our son Ryan's in-laws, Richard and Joan Spitler.

Anfuso Family circa 1950. I'm sitting next to my mom; Frank is on Dad's lap; my sister Maria is in the foreground; Victor and Diana are standing in the rear.

Frank and me as toddlers.

Dad with President John Kennedy outside the Oval Office.

Dad with Vice President Lyndon Johnson.

An earthquake survivor at the stadium in Jacmel, Haiti.

*Me sitting with children in Jacmel, Haiti moments after they sang
"I Am Not Forgotten."*

Colonel Nick Rogers, Bob Craddock and me walking through Grace Village just days after the 2010 earthquake.

Thousands of Haitians, including this young girl, lost limbs as a result of that country's 2010 earthquake.

Doug Coe (center) introducing a friend to President George H. W. Bush.

Photo on my trekking permit for the Everest Base Camp, October 1972.

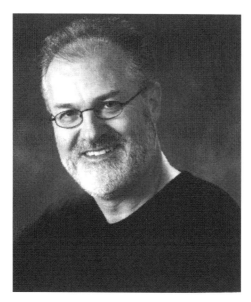

Jim Goll, the prophetic minister who traveled with me to Albania in 1994.

Forward Edge team to Nepal in 1987, fifteen years after my first visit to Nepal in the early '70s. I'm squatting in the back row on the left. Charles Mendies (front row, left) is standing next to our team of sherpas.

A Forward Edge team member at Casa Bernabe, a childrens' home in Guatemala built in the mid-1980s with the help of Forward Edge teams.

Don Tofte (tall blonde in center of back row) leading one of his many FEI mission teams to Tibet. Note the yak-skin boat in the background.

Forward Edge team member offering comfort to a Hurricane Katrina victim in New Orleans.

Members of a Forward Edge team repairing the roof of a damaged home in the Gulf Coast shortly after Hurricane Katrina.

Wilbert Alverado and Gloria Sequiera, directors of Villa Esperanza, a home for at-risk girls from the Managua, Nicaragua landfill.

Dave Watts (r) with Wilbert and Gloria inside La Chureca, Central America's largest landfill.

*Gary Eckelman, the Portland architect who designed Villa
Esperanza, and a member of FEI's board of directors.*

*A group shot of the girls from La Chureca now living in Villa
Esperanza.*

One of the Villa girls, Xochilt, when she was still living in the dump.

Xochilt after three years at Villa Esperanza.

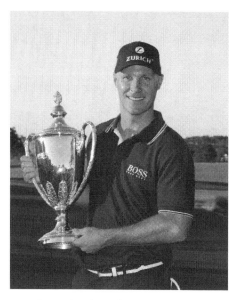

Ben Crane after winning the 2011 McGladrey Classic.

John Wimber, co-founder of the Association of Vineyard Churches.

Bob and Diane Johnson with their three children, Brian, Paige and Monica (bottom left). Bob coordinates all FEI disaster-response teams in the continental United States.

Jeff and Kris Thompson, Forward Edge missionaries in Puerto Cabezas, Nicaragua.

Forward Edge team members helping with rubble removal at Grace Village in Carrefour, Haiti.

An FEI team member caring for a small survivor of the 2010 Haiti earthquake.

Forward Edge Board members, Don and Donna Moen, while leading an FEI team to Kosovo after the Balkan War.

My three amazing children: Ryan (l), Katelyn (c) and Heather (r).

8

LOVE FIRST

....

*"Most of us were taught that God would love us if and
when we change. In fact God loves you so that you can
change. What empowers change, what makes you desirous
of change, is the experience of love. It is the experience of
love that is the engine of change."*

— Richard Rohr

....

YOU MIGHT THINK I'M SPENDING AN inordinate amount of time
on the subject of God's love. But as I've said, a deep, personal
experience of God's love is critical to the process of growing and
enduring as a follower of Christ. It is only God's love that can
satisfy the deepest longings of the human heart, and only God's
love that can free us from our human attempts to meet those
needs by some other means (e.g., money, relationships, religion,
etc.).

Once again, it is often God working through unforeseen events—and our response to those events—that leads to an ever-deepening experience of His love. Not as an end in itself, but as a means of freeing us to share that love with others. It is, in fact, our capacity to receive and share God's love that both determines and signifies the ultimate success or failure of our lives.

OCTOBER, 1994

In the early 1990s, Albania was one of the most unique and fruitful mission fields on earth. Unique, because prior to the fall of the Iron Curtain in 1989 Albania had proudly declared itself "the world's first atheist state." And fruitful, because after forty years of brutally-enforced atheism, the Albanian people were spiritually starving. When the country finally opened its doors again to the outside world, hundreds—even thousands—of Albanians began coming to Christ, and an urgent need arose to nurture the new converts.

I visited Albania in the fall of 1994[18] with a prophetic minister named Jim Goll, who I'd met four months before at that conference in Kansas City. Jim and I had been invited to teach at a fledgling Bible school in Tirana, Albania's capital. I would speak about "The Foundational Truths of the Christian

---

18. This was my third trip to Albania. My first trip had been in 1992, shortly after the fall of communism in Albania.

Faith," while Jim planned to focus on the work of the Holy Spirit—a subject he was not only qualified to teach, but uniquely gifted to demonstrate.

As an only child who grew up on a remote farm in Missouri, Jim developed a close relationship with God at an early age. "I would just talk with Him," he told me on the flight to Tirana. "And He would talk back. It was lonely on the farm, and I had very few friends. Jesus became my friend."

I'd heard numerous stories about Jim and knew that he was frequently used as an agent of serendestiny—his prophetic words often challenging people with messages they had not anticipated or sought. I wondered how God would use him during our time in Albania.

After completing our classes in Tirana, Jim and I accepted an invitation to visit a small town on the Adriatic coast where some residents were showing interest in the claims of Christ. The town was called Sinjin—Albanian for "St. John." Since Albania was situated just across the Adriatic Sea from Italy, and since Christianity had first appeared here sometime in the first century (it was called Ilyrium in the Bible), Jim and I thought Sinjin might have derived its name from a visit by the apostle himself.

Accompanied by a young Albanian believer named Tony, who would be our guide and translator, Jim and I set out for Sinjin in the back of a beat-up Mercedes-Benz sedan—the taxi of choice in most Eastern European countries. The taxi was driven by a stout, mustachioed man named Alex.

As we drove through the Albanian countryside, I was struck

by the barrenness of the landscape and the many reminders of a troubled past: empty factories, thousands of dome-shaped bunkers, and valleys carpeted with tall concrete columns topped by sharp iron spikes.

"They were supposed to impale invading parachutists," Tony explained, referring to the spiked columns. "Hoxha[19] was a very paranoid man."

At last we arrived in Sinjin, a tiny village with one main street and small houses scattered across a steep hillside facing the sea.

"We're meeting in an old movie theater where they used to show propaganda films," Tony told us. "It's the only place in Sinjin large enough."

Alex stayed with the car as the rest of us followed a narrow trail that snaked upward from the street to the most prominent building in town—a warehouse-like structure at the top of the hill. Night was falling, and the first stars were already blinking above our heads.

When we arrived at the theater, we found a ramshackle building covered with peeling red paint, and a crowd of more than one hundred people waiting for us. Men, women and children filled every seat, and another twenty or thirty sat in the center aisle or stood along the walls. Several men huddled near the entrance of the theater, puffing on cigarettes and eyeing

---

19. Enver Hoxha was the leader of Albania from the end of World War II until his death in 1985. Hoxha's leadership was characterized by a not entirely unjustified fear of foreign invaders.

us suspiciously as we passed. The atmosphere was more like a boxing match than a church service.

Tony, Jim and I climbed onto the small stage at the front of the theater. Jim and I had agreed that I would speak first, so without introduction or preamble I stepped to the front of the stage, with Tony beside me to interpret.

"Good evening!" I began. "Thank you for coming tonight."

The buzz of conversations and intermittent laughter persisted. The residents of Sinjin might be interested in Jesus, but they weren't going to make it easy for His followers. Slightly unnerved, I pressed on.

"I want to share with you tonight how the God of the Bible made Himself real to me. I believe He is right here in the room with us tonight, and my friend and I have come from America to make Him known to you."

For the next twenty or thirty minutes I soldiered on, sketching my personal testimony. When I was finished, the noise in the room was, at best, one or two decimals lower than when I'd begun. Reaching people in Sinjin with the gospel was proving harder than I'd expected.

It was then Jim's turn to speak. Unbeknownst to me, Jim had slipped outside the theater while I was speaking so he could pray. He was, after all, accustomed to speaking to God, and to God speaking back. While gazing up at the stars he'd asked God to give him "a word."

Back inside, Jim stepped slowly to the front of the stage. He was silent for several seconds, his brown eyes scanning the crowd, a faint smile fixed in the center of his beard. *What's he up to?* I wondered.

"My friend told you that God is here in the room with us tonight," he finally began. "And I want to prove that to you." He paused. "Is there a woman here named Sarai?"

Several seconds passed before a young woman at the back of the theater cautiously raised her hand. The room became noticeably more quiet.

"Would you please come forward?" Jim asked.

The woman stood at the foot of the stage, her cotton dress falling below her knees and her head wrapped in a lime-colored kerchief.

"You're thirty-one years old, aren't you, Sarai?" Jim asked.

The woman nodded yes. By now, the chatter in the room was barely audible. The audience was watching with curiosity.

"And you have a small lump on your left breast, don't you?"

Another nod, and you could hear a pin drop.

Jim, Tony and I gathered around Sarai to pray for her healing. Before we were finished, ten or fifteen others rushed forward to see if they, too, might be touched by "the living God." For two hours, Jim and I prayed for dozens of people, many opening their hearts to a God who only minutes before had been as foreign to them as the strangers from America. It was without question, one of the most extraordinary "prayer meetings" I have ever experienced.

When the meeting was over, Jim, Tony and I walked back down the shadowy path to the street. I planned to spend another two days in Albania, but Jim had an early-morning flight and was anxious to return to Tirana. Thankfully, Alex's taxi was waiting for us at the curb, and we piled inside.

Still euphoric from our experience in the theater, Jim asked Tony to tell our cab driver what had happened. A surprisingly long conversation ensued, with Alex glancing repeatedly over his shoulder at Jim.

"What's he saying?" Jim finally asked.

"The woman you prayed for, Sarai?" Tony said. "She's Alex's *wife*!"

During the long drive back to Tirana, Jim and I took turns sharing with Alex. By the time he dropped us off, Alex had joined his wife in opening his heart to Jesus Christ. It was the icing on a divinely-concocted cake.

Early the next morning, I found myself lying awake in the apartment where we were staying.

When Jim and I first met, I'd been invited to attend a prayer meeting, which turned out to be in Jim's home. The meeting had opened with Jim asking if anyone needed prayer.

"I need prayer," I'd volunteered.

I then shared with everyone the mysterious dream I'd had—the dream about the house—and how I'd received an interpretation of the dream while showering in my hotel room. "I think the dream was a reminder that God wants a more intimate relationship with me. And that without this, whatever I do in His service is just wood, hay and stubble."

I was surrounded by five or six praying people, including Jim. Many words were spoken, but the ones that stood out most were from Jim: "Love first."

Love first? I remembered wondering at the time. *What does* that *mean?*

But with time it came to me: the Holy Spirit was exhorting me through Jim to overcome my fears of rejection—something I'd struggled with all my life—so I could more freely *initiate* love, regardless of whether or not that love was reciprocated. Letting God love *me*, of course, was a prerequisite. But the more I opened my heart to receive His love, the more capable I'd be of extending that love to others.

Now, as I lay awake in our Albanian apartment, I found my heart brimming with love *for Jim*. What an experience we'd just had! And Jim was the person God had used to make it happen. *I should tell him how much I love and respect him, shouldn't I?*

Just then, Jim's alarm clock went off. He needed to be at the airport by six, and not wanting to disturb me, he went about his business in near-perfect silence.

What should I do? I fretted, pretending to be asleep. *Shouldn't I get up and tell him what a great experience this has been, and how much I love him?* But I held back, unsure what to say or how he would respond.

I was still lying there when I heard the front door of the apartment creak open, then click shut. Jim was gone.

I was overcome with feelings of regret and self-loathing. *You're such a coward*, I thought. *You could have at least told him how much you enjoyed his company.*

Despondent, I swung out of bed and shuffled, barefoot, into the apartment's living room. Slumping onto the threadbare sofa, I reached for my Bible on a nearby end table. My eyes fell on Psalm 42.

"As the deer pants for streams of water,
So my soul pants for you, O God.
My soul thirsts for God, for the living God."

Tears rolled down my cheeks as the words on the page sprang directly into my heart.

"Deep calls to deep in the roar of your waterfalls, all
your waves and breakers have swept over me...
By day the Lord directs his love, at night his song is
with me—a prayer to the God of my life."

I sobbed like a little boy. Once again, I had failed to be an instrument of God's love, to overcome my fears of rejection, to *love first*. But rather than condemning me, God was welcoming me into His arms, letting me know, through Scripture, how much He loved me.

Lord, You're amazing, I marveled, soaking in the presence of His love. *Fill me, Lord, and help me never to forget this moment, so that next time I won't hesitate to give Your love away.*

And so it goes. God revealing His love for us through circumstances we do not anticipate or seek. Not demanding that we change to earn or deserve His love. Instead, loving us first, so that we can love first. Wooing us, guiding us, inviting us into the best story of our lives.

DISCUSSION STARTERS:

❱ How hard or easy is it for you to "love first?"

❱ Read Romans 5:8. Do you think you would be more capable of loving others if you were more certain of God's love for you?

❱ What do you think you could do, if anything, to experience more of God's love?

9

LOVE LETTER FROM GOD

....

"Our spiritual life is a life in which we wait, actively present to the moment, expecting that new things will happen to us, new things that are far beyond our own imagination or prediction. This, indeed, is a very radical stance toward life in a world preoccupied with control."

— Henri Nouwen

....

ANOTHER CRITICAL KEY TO DISCOVERING THE best story of our lives is one we often fail to recognize: *flexibility*. Without flexibility we can easily miss God's plans for us, and as a result, live lives that fall short of His intentions.

While short-term mission trips are, in some respects, a departure from our "normal lives," they can also be a microcosm of our spiritual journeys—a snapshot of what it takes to know God and fulfill His purposes. It is often on a mission trip

95

that people discover the importance of the key I'm referring to here—a discovery that frequently takes place through the phenomenon of serendestiny.

FALL, 2003

We were trying to create a video series to help train our short-term missionaries.

The videos we'd been using for years had grown outdated, and we needed a new way of packaging our training, one that would cover all the bases without being overkill.

Around this time, I found myself circling the enormous maple tree that dominated the front yard of our home. *I need your help, Lord,* I prayed as I paced. *Please, give me an idea that will be practical and effective.*

God rarely answers my prayers right away, but that day, He chose to bless me. As soon as I asked, an unexpected image downloaded into my brain like an attachment from some cosmic computer. I saw God as a vast ocean, steadily sending waves into the shore—each wave representing some aspect of His plan or purposes. I then imagined each wave as a Forward Edge mission trip. *How can people on these trips "catch the wave" of God's plan for them?* I mused.

Again, the answer came as soon as I asked the question. They had to *SURF!* And then the word "surf" morphed into a stunningly-appropriate acronym: S for servanthood, U for unity, R for respect and F for flexibility.

In less than ninety seconds, in a manner I could only explain as supernatural, I received the message for our new video series!

Over the years, more than ten thousand people have been trained with the help of that SURF acronym. And by far the most meaningful letter has been F, for *flexibility*. Without flexibility, a mission team is doomed to failure. Traveling to a foreign country—a place where we have far less control over our day-to-day circumstances than we have back home—*demands* flexibility, and a willingness to let go of our preconceived agendas so we can embrace the unexpected.

The person who embodies this attitude more than anyone I've ever known is my old friend Don Tofte. A former pastor from Hawaii, Don facilitated FEI mission teams to China and Tibet for more than twenty years. Six-feet-four and thin as a rail, Don towered above the average Chinese or Tibetan, but it was his laidback personality, dry sense of humor and ability to go with the flow that made him stand out most, both at home and abroad.

I'll never forget the time Don stood up at one of our annual Forward Edge conferences to read what he called "A Love Letter from God." It was 2002 and Don had just returned from his latest trip. The imaginary letter laid out God's plans for the trip—a kind of preparatory "heads up." Don sub-titled his letter "Looking Back, It All Makes Sense."

> *Aloha, son. Well, another year, another outreach. As you know by now, you plan your course, but I direct your steps. Remember, in your case, the journey is*

your destination. So focus on the people and the events on your way there and back. Okay, here are this year's highlights. Don't forget: be yourself, just somewhere else.

Highlight One. *You will be waiting for a few hours at the Tokyo airport. Kofi Annan [Secretary General of the U.N.] will be on his way to an important meeting regarding the Iraq War. When you see him and his five security guards, you'll be the only other people in the area. Just sit where you are and pray for him, that he'll have wisdom at his upcoming meeting.*

Highlight Two. *When you get to Chengdu [China], I've put seven young people together at an all-night beauty shop. Vern will take a walk and end up there with his guitar, and the rest will fall into place. They'll trim his beard, laugh, sing and dance. He'll be well received as My witness. He'll be gone for over four hours, so don't worry!*

Highlight Three. *When you arrive in Lhasa, you'll meet a thirty-year-old man named Bob who's been diagnosed with AIDs. He's taking a trip to Tibet to "seek the truth." Send Kerry over to meet him in the baggage claim area. A few days later, Kerry will tell him about the Truth he seeks when you meet him again near your hotel.*

98

Highlight Four. *In Lhasa, you'll meet up with the brother of Risan, your Jeep driver from the Everest outreach in 2000. He'll take you to see Risan, who's been seriously ill with high blood pressure. When you arrive at Risan's home, you'll pray for his healing and his salvation. Laugh with him; your visit will cheer him up. He'll listen to you, and so will his wife and daughter. Remember, he saw the JESUS Film on your DVD player at the hotel in Tingri on the way to Everest. He has a TV and DVD player, so show it again so his family can see it, too!*

Note: *Ask your driver, Dopchee, and your guide, Nyma, to keep their eyes open for people with special needs.*

Highlight Five. *On your four-day side trip, you'll stop in Damxung—a small, lonely truck-stop town. There are five young Chinese doctors stationed there. Tell Vern to bring his guitar to the restaurant where they'll be eating dinner. The two interested ones will go back to the hotel with you. Don't freak out when the JESUS Film won't play on your DVD player. The main cord is broken and they don't have time to watch it, anyway. Use one of the hand-cranked cassette players you got from Guy at last year's Forward Edge retreat to play some Bible stories in Tibetan, and give them some literature and tapes. I'll have someone else* *follow up with them next year.*

Highlight Six. *Now pay attention. There's a twenty-year-old Tibetan monk at the Reting Monastery. He's only been there for two months. His eye has a bad infection—you'll spot him right off. Wash out his eye with Visine and tell him to come back before he goes to bed so you can give him some eye medication (use that tube of antibiotic salve you packed at the last minute). In the meantime, you and Kerry spend a few hours with him listening to praise music (watch for his tears). Let him read the Tibetan/ English Bible. He'll soak it up. By the way, he won't be at the monastery next year.*

Highlight Seven. *The next day at Reting Monastery you'll meet some bored monks in the temple. Joke around with them; they're tired of acting spiritual. Eventually let them read one of the Christian tracts you brought. Have the leader chant the tract, and then ask them to sing together. You always wondered if it could be done. Remember to respect the culture!*

Highlight Eight. *On the way to Tidrum Nunnery take note of the sixty-mile stretch of river you're following, and all the little villages along the way. Plan a trip for next year using yak-skin boats. You* *can camp every ten miles or so. The village people will come to you. I'll fill you in later, but expect a hard but exciting outreach. You'll see hail, sickness and death—difficult circumstances, but necessary for the preparation of three team members. One will go on to serve Me in Mexico. Another will do the same in Cairo, Egypt. The third will join YWAM and work on some important projects with David Cunningham, the son of YWAM's founder.*

Highlight Nine. *At Tidrum it will be really cold, but intercede for the people in this area from a nearby mountaintop. Then pour the rest of the oil you've been using for healing prayer into the stream below. Pray that wherever it goes, I go! (Notice that it flows into the big river that goes straight through Lhasa and down into China.)*

Highlight Ten. *Your last stop will be on your way back to Lhasa. Nyma, your guide, will ask you to stop and visit a young woman. (He's been keeping his eyes open like you asked.) She has two deformed legs and has to crawl everywhere. Give her some money (be generous). Nyma and Dopchee will surprise you with their generosity. Then pray for her (one of you can hold her hand). I want her and the whole village to know that she's special to Me. You'll see it in her unusually bright blue eyes. I'll make sure others follow up with* *her, too!*

Remember, Don, to keep listening. Just do your part; be flexible. Don't worry about the circumstances. Just know that I've got a really good plan for you this year, as always.

Love, Jesus.

The names and locales in Don's letter are more exotic than those most of us experience in our day-to-day lives. But all of us face circumstances over which we have no real control, like Don did on his mission trip. We may have plans for our futures, but there are no guarantees that those plans will come to pass.

God has His own plans, His moments of serendestiny for our lives, and only by recognizing and embracing those plans—however unexpected and unwelcome they may appear—can we "catch the wave" of His good intentions. Embracing God's best story for our lives requires flexibility, whether we're serving on a short-term mission team or navigating the more familiar waters of our lives back home.

DISCUSSION STARTERS:

❯ Do you hate surprises? (Be honest.) If so, why do you think that is?

❯ What do you think you could do to take advantage of opportunities that present themselves when things don't go as planned?

10

COMMANDER'S INTENT

....

"If you are avoiding the call of the religious thinking of today's world, and instead are "looking unto Jesus" (Hebrews 12:2) — setting your heart on what He wants, and thinking His thoughts — you will be considered impractical and a daydreamer. But when He suddenly appears in the work of the heat of the day, you will be the only one ready."

— Oswald Chambers

....

I COULD SHARE MANY OTHER STORIES of how flexibility made a powerful difference in the experience of Forward Edge mission teams. But I don't want you to get the impression that flexibility only applies when people are traipsing through a foreign country like Tibet or reaching out to disaster victims in Haiti or Sri Lanka.

More often than not, serendestiny takes place during the course of our everyday lives. And if we're to discover and embrace God's best story for us, we need to expect the unexpected—day in and day out—fixing our minds and hearts on His ultimate intent.

SEPTEMBER, 2010

Ben Crane is one of the best golfers in the world. The son of my friends Doug and Katy (the couple who accompanied me to Sri Lanka after the Indian Ocean Tsunami). Ben loves Jesus, and he and his wife, Heather, have been longtime partners with Forward Edge. Since childhood, Ben has devoted himself to playing golf at the highest level. But golf is not his highest priority.

While on the phone with Doug a few hours after Ben had missed the cut at the 2010 Deutsche Bank Tournament in Boston, Massachusetts, I expressed my sympathy.

"Yeah, that was disappointing," Doug said. "Especially since it probably kills his chances of making the Ryder Cup Team this year. A wonderful thing happened on his way to the airport, though."

"What was that?" I asked, intrigued by the excitement in Doug's voice.

Doug told me that two volunteer drivers had taken Ben and his family to Boston's Logan Airport. Heather rode with their two young children in one car; Ben rode in a second car driven by a guy named Danny. Neither driver had been assigned to the Crane family; they'd simply been tasked with picking up the next group of golfers needing a ride.

"At first, Ben and Danny talked about the tournament, and how disappointed Ben was at missing the cut," Doug explained. "But then Danny began opening up to Ben about his personal life, how he was having problems with his teenage son. The son had recently been hit by a taxi cab while crossing the street, and even though he'd landed on the hood of the cab, he wasn't seriously injured. 'He must have had a guardian angel watching over him,' Danny told Ben.

"That's when Ben starting sharing with Danny the story of his relationship with God. He told him God had a plan for all our lives, and he even gave him some practical advice on how to re-connect with his son. Then he quoted a couple lines from Psalm 57, one of Ben's favorite verses: '...In the shadow of your wings I will take refuge, till the storms of destruction pass by. I cry out to God Most High, to God who fulfills his purpose for me.'

"When they got to Logan, Ben gave Danny a hug and told him to stay in touch. He also gave him his phone number and a copy of the daily devotional he's put together.

"But the coolest thing," Doug concluded, "was that Ben realized if he hadn't missed the cut, he'd never have met Danny. What could have been nothing but a letdown turned out to be the reason for something extraordinary."

"That *is* cool" I told Doug. "It actually reminds me of something I've been thinking a lot about lately. It's called serendestiny...."

After I hung up the phone, I thought about a concept called "Commander's Intent" that we had recently added to the Flexibility section of our training materials. I'd come across the idea in the Continental Airlines in-flight magazine, of all places.

According to the article, the U.S. Army had come up with a simple but highly effective way to prepare troops for battle. Even though the Army had invested huge amounts of time and energy in planning, the article asserted, and even though their policies and procedures had been refined over many years, there was just one drawback: the plans often turned out to be useless.

"The trite expression we always use is 'No plan survives contact with the enemy,'" Colonel Tom Kolditz, head of behavioral sciences at West Point, was quoted as saying. "You may start off trying to fight for your plan, but the enemy gets a vote. Unpredictable things happen: the weather changes, a key asset is destroyed or the enemy responds in a way you don't expect. Many armies fail because they put all their emphasis on creating a plan that becomes useless ten minutes into the battle."

The article went on to describe how in the 1990s the Army changed its planning process, inventing a concept called Commander's Intent (CI). The CI was a clear, plain-talk statement that appeared at the top of every order, specifying the plan's goal—the desired end-state of an operation. It could be something as simple as "Break the will of the enemy in the southwest region," but it never specified so much detail that it risked being rendered obsolete by unpredictable events.

"You can lose your ability to execute the original plan,"

Colonel Kolditz explained, "but you never lose the responsibility of executing the intent."

As I read this, I was struck by how closely it related to real life—and specifically to the phenomenon of serendestiny. In life, we're repeatedly confronted by circumstances we do not anticipate or seek. As Colonel Korditz put it, "Unpredictable things happen." To fulfill our God-given destinies, we must be willing at times to jettison our pre-conceived plans and concentrate instead on our ultimate objective: "God's Intent."

But what *is* God's intent? This is best defined, I believe, by the Westminster Confession of Faith:[20] "Man's chief end is to glorify God, and enjoy Him forever."

And how do we *execute* God's Intent? By making our top priority what Jesus declared in Mark 12:30-31: "The most important [commandment] is this: 'Love the Lord your God with all your heart and with all your mind and with all your strength.' And the second is like unto it: 'Love your neighbor as yourself.'"

During the course of our lives we will often lose our ability to execute our own plans. But we never lose our responsibility to execute God's Intent.

Fulfilling that responsibility, though, can seem virtually impossible when life confronts us with circumstances far more difficult than missing the cut at a golf tournament.

---

20. The Westminster Confession of Faith is a profession of faith that has been influential in Presbyterian churches worldwide ever since it was drawn up in 1646.

DISCUSSION STARTERS:

❯ The Chinese character for the word "crisis" is the same one used for "opportunity." Share an example from your own experience when a personal crisis turned into a positive and unexpected opportunity.

❯ Read Habakkuk 2:14 and 1 Corinthians 10:31. What do you think it means to "do all to the glory of God," and why do you think God wants to fill the whole earth with His glory?

11

THE PET CANARY

"...at the end of your life one of these things will happen to your heart: it will grow hard, it will be broken, or it will be tender. Nobody escapes."

— Ravi Zacharias

MANY YEARS AGO, I HEARD A story that I believe is true, and it's stuck with me ever since. A young woman was cleaning the floors of her apartment when she decided to vacuum the seeds and droppings from her pet canary's cage. Without giving it much thought, she removed the vacuum's nozzle and stretched its long hose attachment into the birdcage.

In the blink of an eye, the tiny canary was sucked into the vacuum hose and disappeared from sight. Panicked, the woman extricated the bird from the vacuum bag and carried it gingerly to the kitchen sink. It took her several minutes to gently wash away the dust and grime from the bird's beak and feathers, and then she returned it to its cage.

A week later, a friend who'd heard about the incident asked how the bird was doing.

"It's really sad," the contrite woman replied. "She doesn't sing anymore. She just sits there, staring into space."

Anyone who's suffered in this life would be quick to confirm that what happened to this canary can also happen to us. Difficult, unforeseen circumstances can rob us of our joy and leave us "staring into space"—and not just for a season, but a lifetime.

Responding with faith, hope and obedience when life "sucks us into its vacuum cleaner" is the most challenging test permitted by the Hand of Serendestiny, and another essential key to embracing God's best story for our lives.

SPRING, 1997

In the spring of 1997, I attended a conference in Denver, Colorado hosted by the Association of Vineyard Churches. The main speaker was the co-founder of the Vineyard Movement, John Wimber. Raised in a non-religious family, Wimber was a gifted musician who's sometimes credited with forming the legendary '60s music group The Righteous Brothers. After years as a beer guzzling, drug abusing pop musician, he became a follower of Jesus in 1963, when he was twenty-nine years old.

I first met Wimber almost twenty years before the Denver conference. I found him to be a sincere, wholehearted follower of

Jesus, with a refreshingly casual style and deep insights into the nature and mission of the Church.

I was also impressed with the growing Vineyard Movement. Birthed during the Jesus Movement of the early 1970s, the first Vineyard home groups drew popular actors and musicians like Bob Dylan. By 1997, Vineyard USA had more than 100,000 members in 500 churches.

In Denver, though, Wimber was in the final stages of a long battle with cancer—a fact that made his messages at the conference uniquely poignant. "Trials and testings are a normal part of the Christian life," Wimber told the assembly. "Our job is to be ready and able to handle the testings with God's help, secure in the knowledge of His care and ultimate delivery."

A burly man with a white beard and gentle demeanor, Wimber was more subdued than when I'd first met him. He'd lost a lot of weight, and his trademark Hawaiian shirt hung loosely around his shoulders and chest.

"One night, just over three years ago," Wimber told the audience, "I woke up with a jolt. 'What is it, Lord?' I wondered. Something in my spirit wasn't right. As the father of four and a grandfather to ten, my immediate thoughts were, 'Is it one of my kids or grandkids?'

"My mouth felt dry, and I had the distinct impression that something frightening was headed my way. Slipping out of bed, I retreated to my prayer corner in the living room and prayed my favorite crisis prayer: '*Oh God, Oh God, Oh God.*'"

A wave of laughter swept through the audience.

"I opened the Bible, expecting the Lord to not only comfort

me but to reveal the nature of this dire warning. He led me to Psalm 33, and I read verse 18: 'But the eyes of the Lord are on those who fear him, on those who hope in his unfailing love.' The next verse perplexed me: '...to deliver them from death and keep them alive in famine.'

"*I'm certainly not starving*, I thought—at the time I weighed two hundred and eighty pounds!"

The crowd offered another wave of respectful laughter.

"I read the rest of the psalm: 'We wait in hope for the Lord; He is our help and our shield.'

"I let out a sigh, relieved to be reminded that God was in charge. He had gotten His message across, though I didn't know what the message was all about. Seven days later, my doctor told me I had cancer."

Wimber went on to describe his radiation treatments, how he'd spent weeks without eating solid food, and how it felt like "walking through the valley of the shadow of death." Gripped by a fear of the unknown, he found himself comforted by the knowledge that he could not plan or control his life—that he had to depend entirely on God.

"Some Christians believe," he continued, "that we should never struggle with doubt or disillusionment or agony. And when we do, it's because we're not exercising the quality of faith we ought to—that periods of disillusionment and despair are sin.

"If those ideas are true," Wimber then said, "then I'm not a good Christian. Not only have I suffered physically with health problems, I've also spent a great deal of time struggling with depression during my battle with cancer. But I've also found that the view from the valley has given me a focus on Christ that I wouldn't have gained any other way. Tragedy, illness, unforeseeable loss and pain will impact all our lives, and while I don't know anyone who would deliberately sign up to suffer so, God uses these experiences to accomplish His purposes in and through us."

Then, to drive his point home, he shared the story of his Christian conversion. It was a slightly different version than ones he'd shared in the past, he confided. His recent illness had given him a fresh appreciation for one character in the story who he sometimes failed to mention.

"I was living at the time in Yorba Linda," he said, "and my life was a mess. I was knee deep in my music career, often performing until the wee hours of the morning. I was also going through a difficult time in my marriage. My wife and I were actually separated. I was ripe for some kind of spiritual awakening, but I didn't know the first thing about Christianity.

"Then one day, I heard a knock on my door. I found a non-descript man standing there with what looked like a Bible in his hand. He said he had some important news to share with me, and asked if he could come in. For reasons I don't understand to this day, I said 'Sure.'

"For the next two hours, this man shared with me about his relationship with Jesus and how the God of the Bible had changed his life. To be honest, I don't really remember much of what he told me, but there was one thing he shared that I will never forget.

"Apparently, this guy had been an elder in a nearby church.

Several years back he and his wife had gone to dinner, leaving their sixteen-year-old daughter home alone. While they were out, someone broke into their home and brutally raped and killed her.

"Naturally, they were devastated. *How could God let this happen to us?* they thought. *Wasn't God supposed to protect us from such things?*

"That night, before going to bed, he said he and his wife were somehow able to kneel beside their bed and pray a simple prayer: 'Lord, we don't understand, but we trust You.'

"He went on to tell me that as time passed God not only restored his faith, but *deepened* it. And how for the past seven years he'd been going door to door, telling people how much God loved them, and that no matter what they experienced in their lives, God was *good*, and that He had a unique and important plan for their lives.

"He pulled a large, tattered map from his pocket and showed me whole sections of Los Angeles that he'd drawn Xs through. 'That's where I've been so far,' he smiled. 'And tonight I ended up here at your door.'

"I didn't become a believer that night," Wimber concluded. "But it sparked a curiosity in me that eventually led me to Christ."

As I listened to Wimber's story, I marveled at the extraordinarily good fruit that had come from two serendestiny moments: the tragic murder of one man's child, and, years later, the unforeseen arrival of that man at John Wimber's door. *What if that girl had not been murdered?* I thought. *And what if her father had not responded with faith and obedience to God's call?*

116

Yes, Wimber might have come to Christ by some other means. But it was far more likely that tens of thousands of people, in the U.S. and around the world, would have never heard the gospel or surrendered their lives to Christ.

As we've seen throughout this book so far, the most significant factor that determines our destinies is how we respond to life's curve balls. A respected pastor cheats on his wife. A sibling commits suicide. A precious toddler drowns in a friend's pool. The tragedies that can strike those who know and love God are endless.

And whenever such things happen—and they invariably do—we are faced with a life-altering decision. Will we harden our hearts and turn away from God? Or will we allow our pain and confusion to sharpen our focus on Christ, "who for the joy set before him endured the cross?"[21] Next to accepting Jesus as our Lord and Savior, these may be the most important spiritual decisions any of us will ever make. The process make take years, and the feelings of pain and loss may last a lifetime, but in the end, we have only three choices: a heart that's hard, a heart that's broken, or a heart that's soft.

---

21. Hebrews 12:2

DISCUSSION STARTERS:

❯ How do you tend to react when unforeseeable tragedy, loss and pain impact your life?

❯ Can you think of a time when God brought an unexpected blessing into your life in the wake of an unforeseen tragedy or loss?

❯ Read 2 Corinthians 1:4. How have you been able to comfort others with the comfort you've received from God? Be specific.

12

KATRINA

"History is a story written by the finger of God."

— Malcolm Muggeridge

WHILE WE'VE SEEN HOW THE PHENOMENON of serendestiny clearly applies to the unfolding of God's plans for us as individuals, it also applies to the destinies of churches, ministries, businesses, even nations.

That's not to say that our own thoughtful planning has no value. It does. But in the end, the success of any organization often has more to do with God working through unforeseen circumstances—and how the leaders of the organization respond to the opportunities they provide—than any humanly-conceived plan.

This has certainly been true for the ministry of Forward Edge.

AUGUST, 2005

When Hurricane Katrina hit the Gulf Coast in August 2005, I knew that God was calling us to respond. Within hours of the first levees breeching, I called an old friend and colleague, Ronny Gilmore, to see if he could travel through the disaster zone to assess the damage and identify potential partners. A former missionary to Guatemala, Ronny was living in Jackson, Mississippi, a short drive from the hardest-hit areas.

"What we need," I told Ronny, "are credible church leaders already reaching out in their communities. We also need facilities where we can base our mission teams."

While we waited to hear back from Ronny, I started to think about how we'd get funding to mount a response. I'd long ago learned that faith preceded provision, in my personal life and in the ministry of Forward Edge. This, in fact, was how we defined "the forward edge:" *When people respond with faith and obedience to God's call—even though they don't know where He's leading or what the outcome will be—they are stepping onto life's forward edge.*

Less than a week after Katrina hit, I received an unexpected phone call from a man named Kay Hiramine, co-founder of a Christian NGO called Humanitarian International Services Group. "We're trying to stand up a coordinated response to Katrina," Kay informed me. "There are several organizations participating, and we'd like Forward Edge to play a lead role."

Two days later, Kay emailed me an impressive strategic plan, twenty-three pages in length, for what he called "The Katrina Response Initiative." Forward Edge was listed as the primary organization coordinating short-term volunteers. I felt honored, but slightly intimidated. *Are we capable of such a responsibility?* I wondered.

I sent Kay's plan to my friend Ron Post, founder and former CEO of the NGO Northwest Medical Teams (now Medical Teams International). I respected Ron's experience with an organization much larger than Forward Edge and was eager to get his feedback.

Three days later, Ron got back to me. "I've reviewed the plan," he began, "and it's very impressive. I'd been praying about how I could help in the Gulf Coast, so when you sent me your plan I passed it on to one of our major donors."

There was a long pause.

"What would you think if we awarded you a million-dollar matching grant so you can execute your part of the plan?"

I was speechless. *A million dollars?* That was almost twice our annual budget!

"Did you say a *matching* grant?" I asked after catching my breath.

"Yes. You'd have to raise a million dollars to get the million dollars. But we can disburse the funds in increments as you raise the money, and the fees and travel expenses of your volunteers can be applied toward the match."

Another long pause.

"Do you think you can do it, Joe?" Ron finally asked.

I didn't answer right away. We'd never raised anything close to a million dollars before. But I knew serendestiny when I saw it, and I trusted, with God's help, that we could meet the terms of the grant.

"Yes," I said, still crunching numbers in my head. "I *know* we can do it."

"Good. Because you're going to have to let the public know about this. Have you ever held a press conference before?"

I hadn't, but one week later I stood in a cavernous warehouse in Portland, preparing for Forward Edge's first-ever press conference. Ron had coached me on how to write a press release, which we'd sent the day before to every major media outlet in Portland. Forward Edge had always "flown under the radar" when it came to public relations, content to build our support base without the aid of mass-media publicity. As a result, we were far from a household name, even in our hometown. *Will anyone show up?* I fretted.

They did. A few minutes before the start of the press conference, three white vans—each sporting satellite dishes and branded with the logo of a local TV station—pulled into the parking lot. I felt like I was dreaming.

It would take more than press conferences, though, to raise a million dollars. Eager for help, I contacted another Portland friend, John Castles, who served as a trustee of a local foundation called Murdock Trust. John was the only person I knew with access to the kind of funding we needed.

"We really need your help," I pleaded. "I know it takes months to get funding from Murdock Trust, but this is *a natural disaster.* People need help now! Is there anything you can do?"

"It doesn't really fit into our areas of interest," John responded graciously. "But I'll see what we can do."

Three weeks later, I was on my way to the Gulf Coast

with one of Murdock's program directors, Terry Stokesbary. According to Terry, the Trust had never sent a program director into the field before, nor had they supported a project outside the five-state region of Alaska, Idaho, Washington, Oregon and California. Our trip, he said, was unprecedented.

Terry and I spent four days in the Gulf Coast, including two days in a devastated New Orleans, meeting with ministry partners and Forward Edge's three volunteer field coordinators, including Ronny, who were already on the ground. They were each either raising their own support or drawing on personal savings. Terry was clearly impressed.

On our return flight to Portland, Terry was careful not to make commitments, and cautioned me not to get my hopes up. "We'll get back to you soon," he said. "Pray."

Five days later, Terry called me at the Forward Edge office. "Unfortunately, we can't help you match the grant," he said.

My heart sunk. *Had we gone all the way across the country for nothing?*

"But there's another way we can help," Terry continued. "We want to increase your capacity as an organization by funding your field staff. We can pay 100% of their salaries for one year, then provide a portion of their salaries, on a declining scale, in years two and three. We can also provide funds to help train them in personal support-raising. That way, when you're finished helping in the Gulf Coast, your missionaries can serve anywhere in the world with Forward Edge."

I was dumbfounded. I'd been so obsessed with matching the million-dollar grant that Murdock's ability to strengthen *our entire organization* had never crossed my mind. It was brilliant.

"Wow, Terry," I said, "that's something I'd never thought of. It sure makes sense, though. I guess there's a reason God entrusts you guys with so much wealth!"

And so, with Terry's help, a proposal was submitted to Murdock Trust for a capacity-building grant of $350,000. Three months later—a time frame much shorter than normal—we received our first disbursement.

In the months and years that followed, God blessed Forward Edge's efforts to serve in the Gulf Coast. With His help—and the help of hundreds of donors—we were able to match the million-dollar grant. And by the end of 2010, more than 3,000 FEI volunteers had helped thousands of Katrina victims return to their homes and places of worship.

In 2009, when full-time field coordinators were no longer needed in the Gulf Coast, two of our field staff, Jeff and Kris Thompson, moved to Nicaragua to help with a safe-water project we'd initiated there, and a third, Bob Johnson, became the coordinator of all our disaster response efforts in the continental United States. Murdock Trust's vision to increase Forward Edge's capacity had become a reality.

Had planning played a role in what happened? Absolutely! Forward Edge was prepared to coordinate short-term volunteers and had people on the ground in the Gulf Coast making connections and exploring opportunities before the flood waters receded.

But it was not our plans that brought success. It was God—intervening in ways we never imagined, opening doors and providing resources far beyond our wildest dreams. It was our willingness to respond with awe and obedience to circumstances we did not anticipate or seek that resulted in a story only *God* could have scripted—a story that honored *Him*, and furthered *His* purposes.

DISCUSSION STARTERS:

❯ When it comes to a church, ministry or business, do you think there's a conflict between making plans and staying open to divinely-orchestrated disruptions of those plans? Elaborate.

❯ Read Psalm 127:1. What do you think this verse means?

❯ Read Proverbs 16:9. Why do you think the maxim "hold your plans loosely" is good advice?

❯ How have you experienced the phenomenon of serendestiny in your church, ministry or business?

JOSEPH ANFUSO

13

THE VILLAGE OF HOPE

"The way of trust is a movement of obscurity, into ambiguity, not into some predetermined, clearly delineated plan for the future...The reality of naked trust is the life of the pilgrim who leaves what is nailed down, obvious and secure, and walks into the unknown without any rational explanation or guarantee for the future. Why? Because God has signaled the movement and offered it his presence and his promise."

— Brennan Manning

THERE'S A REASON THE BIBLE CALLS Abraham "the father of all those who believe"[22]—he lived *by faith*. When God told him

---

22. Romans 4:9-12

to "go to the land I will show you,"[23] he obeyed, even though he had no clue where he was going or what awaited him there. "This is why it was credited to him as righteousness. [And] the words 'it was credited to him' were written not for him alone, but also for us...who believe in him who raised Jesus from the dead."[24]

If we're to discover the best stories of our lives, we must be willing, like Abraham, to leave behind what is safe and familiar, and follow God into the unknown. This is the hallmark of serendestiny—the path of ambiguity that leads to the future He has planned for us.

FALL, 2007

In the fall of 2007, Forward Edge's field coordinator in Nicaragua was a twenty-something woman named Gloria Sequeira. Gloria's job was to identify Nicaraguan partners, primarily orphanage directors and school principals, with whom our mission teams could serve. She had a heart filled with love and compassion, and she was good at what she did.

Two years before, Gloria's heart had led her to *La Chureca* (The Wastebasket), a community of approximately two thousand people living inside Managua's main landfill. She formed friendships with families in *La Chureca*, who all survived by

---

23. Genesis 12:1

24. Romans 4:22-25

salvaging from the dump. Young girls were the most vulnerable, often sold as prostitutes to the truck drivers who brought in the garbage. The more Gloria learned about the horrors inside the dump, the more she wanted to help.

At first, Gloria arranged for FEI mission teams to serve at a Christian school inside the dump, ministering to the children and making needed improvements. The service of these teams was helpful and much appreciated. But Gloria knew that neither the school nor the visiting mission teams could protect the *La Chureca* children from abuse, and it broke her heart. What Gloria didn't know was that God was about to arrange a series of serendestiny moments that would not only change her life, but the lives of dozens of *La Chureca* children.

It started during a visit by a young man, Sam Martin, who Forward Edge sent to Nicaragua to make a video about Gloria's ministry inside the dump.

Sam asked Gloria, "If money were no object, what would you do to help the girls of *La Chureca*?"

Without hesitating, Gloria said, "I'd get them out of there!"

Sam returned to the States and shared this with me, and I knew at once that God was calling us to support Gloria's vision. With His help, I was convinced that we could raise enough money to build a safe haven for the *La Chureca* girls, far from the horrors of the dump. I was also convinced that we needed more than just money.

Sam's parents, Jeff and Liz Martin, hosted a Christmas party in their home shortly after Sam returned to the States, and they invited Karen and me to attend. Jeff and Liz had heard about the girls in *La Chureca* and Gloria's vision to rescue them, and they wanted me to meet someone they thought could help—a Portland architect named Gary Eckelman.

"I'm heading to Nicaragua in a few weeks and would love for you to join me," I told Gary during a long conversation that night. "We could use someone with your talents."

Nicaragua? I could almost hear Gary thinking. *Why would I want to go there?*

"Well, maybe," Gary replied. "I'll think about it."

Several days later, Gary called me. "I'll go with you," he said, a hint of uncertainty in his voice. "But I can't commit to anything."

Five weeks later, Gary and I were in Nicaragua, accompanied by a seventy-something business owner from Colorado named Dave Watts.

Gary's first serendestiny moment—apart from the invitation to visit Nicaragua—came during his first visit to *La Chureca*. Gloria and her husband, Wilbert, drove Gary, Dave and I to the dump. It was Gary's first time in a Third World country, and I was anxious to see how he would respond.

As Wilbert steered the van down a narrow lane, we passed men, women and children covered in soot, many with sacks over their shoulders, plodding along the roadside like prisoners in a concentration camp. All around us, fires flared in mountains of foul-smelling trash. As we got closer to the heart of the dump, we could see more men, women and children sifting through the trash as a squadron of buzzards circled eerily overhead. Here and there, crude wood and tin shelters indicated that the scavengers were not just visitors to the dump, but permanent residents.

Gloria tapped Wilbert on the shoulder and told him to stop the van. Rolling down her window, she called out to a girl standing beside a trash pile. Despite her matted hair and dirt-smeared face, the girl was strikingly beautiful. She appeared to be in her early teens.

"Ileana!" Gloria called.

Expressionless, the girl stepped slowly toward the van. Gloria told her something in Spanish—something Dave, Gary and I could not understand. I could tell from Gloria's tone, though, that she was offering words of loving exhortation. But the girl did not respond; she stared blankly at the ground, her face a mask of resignation. When Gloria had finished speaking with her, the girl slowly backed away and returned to the trash pile.

"What did you say to her?" Gary asked from the back of the van.

"I'm concerned for her," Gloria replied, staring out the window, not answering Gary's question directly. "She's been sleeping with the truck drivers since she was ten. Now she's living with a man in his fifties. I was hoping we could save her, but now I'm not sure."

Gary, Dave and I sat silently for several minutes.

"Hey, Gary," Dave suddenly said. "You go to a big church in Portland, don't you? Why don't you ask your pastor if he'd take up an offering so we can buy land and get these girls out of here? If he does that, Gary, I'll match it, dollar for dollar."

Gary did not respond. *What's he thinking?* I wondered. He

was quiet for the rest of his visit.

Two days later, just before we returned to the States, I asked Gary point blank if he was willing to design a home for the *La Chureca* girls.

"I knew the moment I saw Ileana," he said. "She broke my heart. Yes, I'll design the home for you. And I'll see if I can get my pastor to take up an offering, too."

Four weeks later, I called Dave in Colorado.

"Hey, Dave, guess what?"

"What?"

"Gary's pastor took up that offering."

"Great!" Dave whooped. "How much was it?"

"Are you sitting down?"

"No, but go ahead…how much was it?"

"It was $87,000."

There was a long pause.

"Did you say $8,700?"

"No, Dave. Eigh-ty-se-ven- *thou*-sand dollars."

There was another long pause. Dave was not stingy or lacking in faith, but he wasn't Bill Gates or Warren Buffet, either.

"Okay," Dave finally said. "I told Gary I'd match the offering, and I'm a man of my word. I'll have to send it to you in increments, though. God loves those girls more than we do. I'm confident He'll provide."

And so, Gloria's dream for a home for girls in the Managua dump became a reality. The offering from Gary's church (SouthLake Foursquare), combined with Dave's match, was exactly what we needed to buy two acres of land on the outskirts of Managua. We dubbed the property *Villa Esperanza,* or Village of Hope, and Gary designed a wonderful neighborhood of homes, guest houses and outbuildings to be built there.

In the weeks and months that followed, other donors would step up to help. On July 10, 2008, the first sixteen girls from the Managua dump took up residence. By 2010, twenty-four girls were living at *The Villa,* and plans were underway to add another twenty-four in the months and years to come.

How had all this happened? Not through our carefully conceived plans. It was God, drawing together an unlikely band of ordinary people who embraced their serendestiny moments: first Gloria, who responded with faith to Sam's unexpected question; then Gary, who accepted my out-of-the-blue invitation to visit Nicaragua and Dave's challenge to ask his pastor to take an offering; and finally Dave, who when confronted by the unforeseen task of donating a huge sum of money had stepped up and kept his word.

It was serendestiny that led to the realization of Gloria's dream. Yes, it would take planning to construct *The Villa,* and more planning to pursue its long-term mission. But without serendestiny there would have been no Villa, and far less reason to give God the glory.

But discovering one's destiny takes more than just responding with faith and obedience to God's call. As we will see in the next chapter, it also takes a willingness to *appreciate* whatever that call might be. Sadly, it's our unwillingness to rejoice in God's plans for us that often thwarts His good intentions, and keeps us from embracing the best story of our lives.

DISCUSSION STARTERS:

❯ Read 1 Corinthians 3:10-15. Do you think it's possible for followers of Christ to do genuinely good works without God receiving any glory? Explain.

❯ Read Acts 16:6-10. Why do you think it's important to allow God to guide or even interrupt our plans?

❯ What attitudes and/or behaviors have sometimes prevented your good deeds from bringing glory to God?

14

WHAT IS SUCCESS?

....

"Lord, you have assigned me my portion and my cup;
You have made my lot secure.
The boundary lines have fallen for me in pleasant places;
Surely I have a delightful inheritance."

— Psalm 16:6

....

IT SHOULD BE APPARENT BY NOW that I did not always believe David's words, that "the boundaries [had] fallen for me in pleasant places." For many years, I'd struggled with feelings of inferiority. I doubted that I could measure up to the worldly success of my father, or the physical and social gifts of my twin.

What I didn't realize was that *most* people—even the most seemingly "successful"—struggle with not feeling good enough. There's always someone smarter, more accomplished, more passionate or spiritual. The Bible is filled with stories of those who compared themselves with others: Saul envied David,[25] the brothers of Joseph sold him into slavery,[26] Leah resented Rachel[27] and Cain killed Abel.[28]

I've come to believe that the only antidote for human feelings of inferiority is a decision to believe, confess and act in accordance with the following truth: *"For we are God's workmanship, created in Christ Jesus for good works which God prepared in advance for us to do."*[29]

Every person's life is rich with the promise of meaning, purpose and indescribable delight. Every one of us has a story. And it is often serendestiny that helps us believe, appreciate and eventually fulfill the reality of that promise.

APRIL, 2008

Approximately three months before the opening of *Villa Esperanza*, I attended an invitation-only CEO retreat in Seattle sponsored by AERDO, the Association of Evangelical Relief and Development Organizations.

On the three-hour drive from Vancouver to Seattle, I found myself reflecting on a conversation I'd had recently with Donna

---

25. 1 Samuel 18:8-9

26. Genesis 37:12-28

27. Genesis 30

28. Genesis 4:1-16

29. Ephesians 2:10

Moen, a Forward Edge board member and the wife of our board president. Donna had a unique way of looking at things and a deep commitment to the vision and values of Forward Edge. She and Don had led numerous FEI mission teams over the years, and I not only considered them pillars in the Forward Edge family but among my closest friends.

I'd called Donna for advice about a tension I felt about the future direction of Forward Edge. We'd been growing in recent years, and a consultant we'd contracted was trying to convince me that refined branding and a more sophisticated approach to donor development would accelerate that growth. But was that what we wanted? I had no problem with the concept of growth if it allowed us to do more of the ministry we were called to, but I was concerned that if we grew too big we might lose, or at least weaken, the organizational values I'd come to cherish: close relationships, a staunchly non-corporate culture and a responsiveness to the Holy Spirit.

"I feel like I'm being pulled in two directions," I told Donna. "On one hand, if we were bigger we could help more people. On the other, I'm worried that if we get *too* big we could end up compromising our DNA."

Donna had understood. She'd always valued Forward Edge's DNA—informal, relational, non-corporate. We'd even joked in the past about giving her a business card with the title "Guardian of the Guts."

"You know, the whole time you've been talking," Donna told me, "I had this mental picture—a picture of two ladders, one really tall, the other one shorter. You're standing on the shorter ladder, but one of your legs is stretching out toward the taller one.

"I think what this means is that you need to be careful not to reach for something God hasn't called you to," she told me. "The ladder you're on is a *good* ladder, Joseph. You need to appreciate what you have."

As I drove toward Seattle, Donna's comment kept rattling around in my head. *Appreciate what you have...appreciate what you have...appreciate what you have....*

I arrived at the retreat, which would take place in a mansion modeled on a medieval English manor house. Once the estate of former Boeing president Philip Johnson, it consisted of fourteen neatly-manicured acres and boasted a sweeping view of the Puget Sound. I was properly intimidated, and considered it a fitting gathering place for the notable company I was about to enter.

As FEI's president, I had the necessary credentials to participate in the retreat. But since most of the CEOs attending ran organizations much larger than Forward Edge, I could not help but feel slightly intimidated. Among the attendees were the presidents of two of the largest Christian ministries in the world—men who, out of respect, I will simply call Mr. Green and Dr. Blue. Prior to assuming leadership of Organization X, Mr. Green had been the CEO of an international corporation overseeing four thousand employees and $500 million in annual sales. Dr. Blue had been raised on the mission field, and held a PhD from a prestigious university in the Midwest. Both ran organizations with annual budgets in excess of $1 billion—

nearly one hundred times the budget of Forward Edge. As was often the case with me, interacting with people like this, whose personal narratives did not include my years of aimlessness, triggered old feelings of insecurity, and I feared either disappearing in their presence or overcompensating by coming on too strong.

I'm not going to say much, I vowed as I pulled my car into the mansion's parking lot. *Better to just be a fly on the wall.*

After a lavish breakfast prepared by Dominican nuns who lived at the estate, the twenty or so retreat attendees gathered around a large table in a wood-paneled room with ornate plaster ceilings and a grand fireplace. Mr. Green sat at one end of the table; Dr. Blue sat near the middle, directly across from me. After another attendee opened the meeting with prayer, Mr. Green suggested that we get to know each other better by sharing our favorite musicians. "Bob Dylan, Patty Griffin and Fernando Ortega," I said when it was my turn.

Mr. Green then asked a more serious question: "We are leaders of *faith-based* relief and development agencies. How can we keep our organizations from drifting away from Christ?"

A lively discussion ensued, filled with sincere and helpful suggestions: prayer, transparency, mutual accountability, monthly Bible studies, etc. As the discussion continued, I could feel my heart starting to pound in my chest. It was the feeling I knew well by then, the same sense of urging I'd felt in that living room in India two years before. The Holy Spirit wanted me to speak.

I forsook my "fly-on-the-wall" vow and jumped into the

conversation.

"I think we all have deep needs for approval and significance," I began. "We also live in a culture that touts the idea that bigger is better. Because of this, I think we have a tendency to assume that growing our organizations—making them as big and far-reaching as possible—is a kind of given, that this should automatically be one of our priorities. But if we do that, if we just assume we're supposed to get bigger and bigger, we might end up with large organizations, but God may not be in the picture anymore. Look at the Ivy League colleges," I concluded. "They started out training ministers, but now they're almost uniformly *hostile* to the Christian faith."

As I made my remarks, I noticed a disapproving frown on Dr. Blue's face. *I knew I should have kept my mouth shut*, I thought.

No sooner had I finished, in fact, then Dr. Blue, misunderstanding my comment, took me to task. "I disagree," he said. "The world needs ten or twenty billion dollar ministries committed to serving the poor. Big is not bad. There's a big, hurting world out there, and without resources there's not much we can do to help."

My fears have come upon me, I groaned inwardly. *Open mouth, insert foot.*

"Ah…no, that's not what I meant, Dr. Blue…" I started to defend myself.

"I think I know what Joe means," Mr. Green interjected. "Mother Teresa was once asked to share the secret of her success. 'God didn't call me to be successful,' she answered. 'He called me to be *faithful*.'"

"Yes, that's what I meant," I said, nodding and smiling at Dr. Blue. "I wasn't suggesting that big is bad, just that big shouldn't be our ultimate goal."

There was a moment of silence. Dr. Blue nodded and graciously returned my smile.

And so, with the timely help of Mr. Green, I managed to dodge a well-intentioned bullet. I had also affirmed—in my own heart, at least—a vital truth about God's best story for our lives: it doesn't matter how grand His plans for us may seem, or how those plans look to someone else. If it's *God's* plan, it's GRAND—regardless of how small or seemingly insignificant it may appear. Only when we truly believe this can we rest and rejoice in the knowledge that "the boundaries have fallen for [us] in pleasant places."

Comparing ourselves with others may be the single most common reason too few believers discover and pursue God's unique plans for them. Overcoming this temptation is a critical key to embracing serendestiny and discovering the best story of our lives.

DISCUSSION STARTERS:

❯ Why do you think we sometimes make the mistake of trying to assess the value of what God has called us to in His service?

❯ Read 2 Corinthians 10:12. Has comparing yourself with others ever prevented you from making a contribution to God's purposes? If so, explain.

❯ What perspective(s) do you think you'd need to have to avoid comparing yourself with others?

15

BUTTERFLIES

> *"Self-rejection is the greatest enemy of the spiritual life because it contradicts the sacred voice that calls us the "Beloved." Being the Beloved constitutes the core truth of our existence."*

— Henri Nouwen

ONE OF MY FAVORITE TV PROGRAMS is *Antiques Roadshow*. I know, I'm a geek. But I not only find unique, historically significant objects fascinating, I'm also deeply moved— sometimes even to tears—when the owners of these objects discover that what they've been holding onto for years is worth far more than they ever imagined. Like the woman who learns the mahogany chair in her grandmother's attic is worth $80,000-$120,000, or the lady who discovers the Gibson mandolin her grandfather paid twenty bucks for during the Great Depression is now valued at $175,000. Or the elderly man who's told the Navajo blanket handed down in his family for generations would bring $350,000-$500,000 at auction. "I had no idea," I remember the old man exclaiming. "It was just leaning on the back of a chair."

Not long ago, I had my own *Roadshow* experience while watching a 2012 episode filmed in Tulsa, Oklahoma. I was sitting in our family room when a woman with two paintings of brightly-colored butterflies appeared on the screen.

We have one of those! I gasped, hardly believing my eyes.

I stood up and looked behind the door. There, covering an unsightly hole where an old wall sconce once hung, was a numbered print of the very same painting—a watercolor by the French artist E.A. Seguy. Given to us by a friend, the painting had been hanging behind that door—virtually unseen—for more than twenty years.

I lifted the painting from the wall and rushed back to the sofa to listen for the appraiser's estimate. "They're a fine example of early Art Deco design," he concluded, "and worth $2,000 each."

As I stared at the long-ignored, and now valuable, painting in my hands, I understood why I loved *Antiques Roadshow*. It was the connection I made between objects that seemed worthless to their owners and the countless people, including Christians, who underestimate their value as creatures made in God's image. "For we are God's *masterpiece*," Scripture declares. "He has created us anew in Christ Jesus, so we can do the good things He planned for us long ago."[30]

You may struggle, as I've shown you that I did, to apply this truth to your personal life. But once you have—once you've

---

30. Ephesians 2:10 New Living Translation (NLT)

appropriated the value and purpose this truth imparts to you—your life can never be the same. No longer will you question your worth in God's sight, or doubt that you have a part in His purposes. On the contrary, you'll be energized by the realization that God made you, just the way you are, to participate in His eternal plans.

Significantly, this realization often comes to us through circumstances we do not anticipate or seek.

OCTOBER, 1995

Throughout much of her life, my wife Karen has struggled with feelings of insignificance. As the third-born of nine children, Karen often felt invisible. "Whenever our family was introduced to people," she told me early in our relationship, "I was just 'one of the Brennan kids.' Sometimes our closest family friends had trouble remembering our names."

Even after coming to Christ in her early twenties, Karen's feelings of insignificance persisted. "I guess I have the gift of encouragement," she would sometimes say, as if it had little or no value. "Big deal."

In the fall of 1995, God orchestrated an event that would profoundly alter Karen's self image. It happened at a Christian retreat called "Consequential."

One of the stated purposes of the retreat was to help attendees develop more fruitful and authentic relationships with God and with others. I wanted to attend because of my desire to keep growing as a follower of Christ. Karen, on the other hand, had a different motivation. Although I didn't know it when we arrived, she had concerns about our marriage and hoped the retreat would provide a breakthrough.

During a freewheeling discussion on the retreat's opening day, I was seated next to Karen in a circle of fifty or sixty people. The topic of the discussion was "What Struggles Are You Facing in Your Relationships?"

"I love my husband," Karen suddenly blurted. "But sometimes he can be hard of hearing. Over the years, when I've tried to caution him about something or give him some helpful advice, he blows me off and keeps on doing what he's doing. It's like he's got wax in his ears."

I was embarrassed. *Did she have to tell everyone in the room?* But honesty and directness were qualities I'd always admired in Karen, and I soon learned that they were qualities many others in the room admired, too.

Over the weekend, we participated in numerous other discussions, as well as a series of thought-provoking exercises. After Karen's first outburst, I talked more than she did during the discussions, but she interacted more freely during the informal breaks, frequently sharing words of affirmation with other participants.

On the retreat's final day, the retreat facilitator, a stocky Italian-American named Mike, guided us through an exercise he called "The Lifeboat." After gathering us in a circle, he told us to imagine ourselves as passengers on a sinking ship. The ship had just one lifeboat, with a maximum seating capacity of eight. He then gave each of us eight popsicle sticks.

"I want you to go around the room and hand out your sticks," Mike instructed. "I want you to give them to the eight people you would trust the most to communicate to your family and friends how much you loved them. And remember, these will be the only eight people who survive the sinking ship."

We all surveyed the fifty or sixty people in the room. Most of us would not "survive" the sinking ship. For the next fifteen or twenty minutes, we circled the room, distributing our sticks. When the exercise was nearly over, Mike asked me how many sticks I had.

I counted twelve. *Not bad*, I thought.

"And how many sticks does Karen have?" he asked.

I glanced across the room. To my surprise, I saw thirty or forty sticks sprouting from Karen's hands like a wooden bouquet—more, in fact, than anyone else in the room.

"I think Karen's got some golden nuggets for you, Joe," Mike whispered in my ear. "You'd be wise to pay more attention to her."

For Karen, it was a serendestiny moment. The sticks in her hands confirmed how precious she was in God's sight, and in the sight of others. It was also an eye-(and-ear)-opening experience for me. From that day forward, I saw Karen in a whole new light. I realized, more deeply than ever before, that God had placed her in my life to bless me—and others—with golden nuggets of wisdom. In the years that have followed, I've watched with admiration and respect as Karen beat back the lies of the enemy to share words of truth and encouragement with countless people in need, including me. Much the way serendestiny had exposed the lie of being "less than" in my life (Jim DeGolyer's prophecy about the two babies) God had used serendestiny to expose the lie of insignificance in Karen's.

I once heard a Roman Catholic priest say, "It's impossible for God to be disappointed with us. Disappointment comes when we have an image of someone and then find out they don't live up to that image. But God doesn't see us based on an image. He sees who we *really* are—who *He* made us to be—and that is the person He loves."

I have often wondered what the Body of Christ would be like if every member knew his or her worth in God's sight. What if every "chair," forgotten in some dusty attic, became a lap where weary pilgrims could sit and rest? If every "mandolin," long silent in its case, made life-giving music for the disillusioned and downcast? If every "blanket," just leaning on the back of a chair, instead offered warmth to the lonely and unloved? And every "butterfly," rather than hiding behind a door of lies, took flight again, bringing beauty into a world starved for grace?

Wherever we are in our journeys, we can find hope and comfort in these timeless words of Jesus: "If you abide in my word, you are truly my disciples, and you will know the truth, and the truth will set you free."[31] As we've seen, it's a promise that often becomes real and transformational for us through the phenomenon of serendestiny.

---

31. John 8:32

DISCUSSION STARTERS:

❱ How has the truth of Ephesians 2:10 impacted your life, if at all? Please be specific.

❱ Read 1 Corinthians 12:21-26. Why do you think these verses are included in Scripture?

❱ What are some practical ways you could bestow greater honor on those in the Body of Christ you might think of as "less honorable"?

JOSEPH ANFUSO

16

PENCILS

....

"We are all pencils in the hand of a writing God, who is sending a love letter to the world."

— Mother Teresa

....

YEARS AGO, I WATCHED A DOCUMENTARY on the life of Mother Teresa. One of the most striking scenes was an interview with a nun who'd supervised Mother Teresa during her early years in India, back when she was a teacher at a small convent school in Calcutta.

"What do you remember about her in those days?" the interviewer asked, clearly expecting to hear something remarkable about the future Nobel Peace Prize winner.

The nun did not answer at first. She seemed surprised, perhaps even a bit embarrassed. "Well, I don't actually remember her," she finally stammered. "She was just one of the nuns."

It was an entirely believable response. There was nothing about Mother Teresa that made her stand out among her peers. At four-foot-ten and not inclined to draw attention to herself, she was not someone who seemed destined for greatness.

But God delights to use ordinary people. Consider the many obscure and seemingly insignificant characters highlighted in Scripture: Dorcas, the early disciple who made clothes for the poor, and who Peter raised from the dead;[32] Abishag, the "young virgin" who cared for the dying King David;[33] the unnamed slave girl who prompted the healing of King Naaman;[34] and the boy who brought five loaves and two fishes that would end up feeding thousands.[35]

God not only uses ordinary people, he sometimes uses people you and I might have easily disqualified: murderers (Saul); prostitutes (Rahab); adulterers (King David); and deceivers (Jacob). Sinners, in fact, were among Jesus' favorite companions.[36]

The truth is, God longs to use each of us, regardless of our past failings, our physical appearance or our meager station in life. We are *all* pencils in the hand of a writing God. And the stories He wants to tell through us are often revealed through circumstances we do not anticipate or seek.

---

32. Acts 9:36-42

33. 1 Kings 1:1-4

34. 2 Kings 5:1-19

35. John 6:9-14

36. Mark 2:15-17

★   ★   ★   ★

The coordinator of all Forward Edge domestic disaster-response teams is a man named Bob Johnson. With his shoulder-length hair, a ready smile and easygoing personality, Bob is the personification of "a regular guy." His background, however, is anything but regular.

I want to share Bob's story with you, written in his own words. Like the story of every Christ follower, it's a story of redemption. A story of grace. A story of serendestiny.

"I don't have a clue who my biological father is. My mom was married and divorced many times, and the man I thought was my father split when I was seven. Mom liked to drink at parties, and I have a hard timing remembering a time when she was sober.

"I had my first run-in with the law when I was eight. That's when I started running away. By the age of thirteen, I was using drugs and alcohol pretty regularly, and by fourteen I'd committed my first felony, stealing from a local business. When I was fifteen I was placed in the Guardian Angel Home in Joliet, Illinois—a Catholic facility for troubled youth. I lived there until I was eighteen.

"By my early twenties I was pretty much homeless and living a life of crime, bouncing around from hotels to friends' houses to cars. When I was twenty-three, I was arrested and charged with my fifth felony for commercial burglary. As a repeat offender in Illinois, I faced a mandatory sentence of thirty years. And my sentencing judge was so tough he was known as 'a hanging judge.'

"I was basically a skinny white kid who was on his way to prison for a long, long time.

"Then something amazing happened. The judge agreed to waive my prison sentence if I was willing to go to drug treatment. Naturally, I agreed.

"In treatment, my first moment of clarity came when the counselor asked our group what the first step in the AA program was. Forty-eight men replied in unison: 'I was powerless over alcohol, and my life had become unmanageable.'

"'You're wrong,' the counselor said. 'Try again.'

"Then one guy in the corner said, '*WE* were powerless....'

"I didn't hear anything after that. The word 'we' made me realize that for the first time in my life I was part of something bigger than myself. For the first time in my life, I wasn't alone.

"That's what started me down the road to recovery. It took about another year before I finally surrendered my life to Christ after an AA meeting. Then I started to go to informal Bible studies.

"I married Diane in 1995. I already had two sons from a previous relationship, Brian and Billy. Paige was born in 1996, and Monica followed two years later.

"In 2000, I went on my first mission trip to the Perkins Foundation in Jackson, Mississippi. They were involved in inner-city work—education, housing, job creation, Bible studies. We helped build volunteer housing for them.

"Fast forward to 2004, when Florida got nailed by seven hurricanes. We were praying about this at church one Sunday, and I got the conviction that I needed to go do hurricane relief work. At the end of the service, I turned to Diane and said, 'We need to talk.'

"When we got home, I told Diane what I was feeling and that we needed to leave in the morning.

"Now, Diane is a planner. The first thing she said was, 'We need a plan.' I had a painting business, and we had to find a few people to cover for us while we were gone. So that night we made some phone calls, and several friends stepped up to help. We left Tuesday morning instead of Monday.

"My decision to leave for Florida was confirmed when our church took up an offering to help cover our expenses. We hadn't asked them to do this, and the offering wasn't actually taken up until *after* we'd left. But there was so much excess that I was able to go back to Florida for an extra two weeks.

"When Hurricane Katrina hit, I was swamped with business but had very little cash on hand. I didn't think I could go. Some friends at church were putting together a team, though, and asked for my advice. By the end of the week, everyone said, 'Get in the truck.' So I did.

"While I was on the trip, I was in charge of daily devotions. One day, when I was preparing for the next day's devotions, God spoke to me: 'You're gonna come back down here in two weeks, and stay for six months.' It was the one time in my life when I heard the voice of God clearly.

"I fought it. I had a business to run, a family to support, a life I needed to take care of. But I kept getting up in the middle of the night and reading the Bible. One night I came across

Matthew 6:28, the verse about the lilies of the field. It was two in the morning, and I said, 'Okay, God, I'll go. But You need to tell my wife.'

"I fell asleep and woke up at 5:30, completely refreshed. I called my pastor and told him what had happened. He came over to my house and grilled me. He wanted to make sure this was a call, not just compassion. At the end of the meeting, he sent me out with his blessing and the blessings of the church.

"I was back in the Gulf Coast within two weeks and stayed for six months, just like God said. Diane and the kids joined me. I was working with the Perkins Foundation at the time, coordinating their volunteer teams.

"At the end of the six months, we went home. It tore me up to leave. There were still so many people who needed help. So that Christmas I went back down again for a week.

"That's when I met David Botha, one of Forward Edge's field coordinators. He told me Forward Edge was looking for more field staff in the region, so when I got home I called the Forward Edge office in Washington and spoke with Joe Anfuso. I already knew God was sending me; I was just waiting for Joe and the other Forward Edge leaders to say 'yes.'

"Two months later, I flew out to the West Coast to meet with Joe. We had a long conversation, and at the end of the meeting Joe said I was part of the team.

"Diane, the girls and I arrived back on the Coast in June, and stayed for almost two years. We worked with teams from across the country, helping dozens of people return to their homes. One thing I always made sure to do was tell my story. I wanted those short-term missionaries to know that their leader was going to be transparent, and I hoped they would be, too.

"Since returning from the Gulf Coast, I've been working with Forward Edge as the field coordinator for all domestic disaster-response teams. I've been to Houston, Nashville, Alabama, Kentucky and Joplin, and many times back to New Orleans.

"Looking back, I have to laugh. God must have a real sense of humor to take me from where I was to where I am today. Some of my past may be ugly, but I would never have known the love and grace of God the way I do now if I hadn't come up that way. I guess God can use anyone if they're willing to hand their lives over to Him, and if they're willing to say 'yes' when He calls."

I'll never forget sitting with Bob when he flew out to Washington to interview for the job. I admit that I wondered at the time if adding Bob to our team was a good idea. How would some team members, group leaders and pastors feel if they knew a guy with Bob's background was coordinating their mission trip?

But a voice deep inside kept whispering to me as I listened to Bob's story. *You're not so different from him. You were homeless once, you used drugs, you were lost and alone with no real purpose in life. You're no better than this guy.*

I have never once regretted adding Bob to the Forward Edge team. In fact, he's one of our stars. The people who facilitate FEI mission teams include firemen, policemen, health-care professionals, successful business owners, pastors and school superintendents. But no one receives more favorable reviews than Bob Johnson: the former substance abuser, the five-time felon, the skinny white kid on his way to prison, the pencil in the hand of a writing God.

DISCUSSION STARTERS:

❱ What serendestiny moments did you notice in Bob's story?

❱ Read 1 Corinthians 1:26. Why do you think God delights to use ordinary people?

❱ How do you think Bob's story might relate to God's plan for *your* life?

17

GOD'S TIMING

....

*"A saint's life is in the hands of God like a bow and arrow
in the hands of an archer. God is aiming at something the
saint cannot see, but our Lord continues to stretch and
strain, and every once in a while the saint says, 'I can't
take it any more.' Yet God pays no attention; He goes on
stretching until His purpose is in sight, and then he lets the
arrow fly."*

— Oswald Chambers

....

GOD OFTEN REVEALS HIS PLANS FOR us more slowly than we'd
prefer. This, I believe, is for at least two reasons: first, if we knew
in advance what He had planned, we might turn down His
invitation to follow; and second, fully accomplishing His plan
will likely require more confidence in His goodness—and more
humility—than we presently possess. Regardless of the reasons,

fulfilling God's plans for us almost always takes *time*.

There are, of course, many biblical examples: Abram (later Abraham) did not leave Ur until the age of seventy-five;[37] Joseph became his country's leader only after years in an Egyptian dungeon;[38] Caleb did not enter the promised land until the age of eighty-five;[39] and Moses, after forty years in the desert, finally heard God's call at the age of eighty.[40]

Even those who hear God's call at an early age and enter quickly into ministry invariably face challenges and growing responsibilities that require an ever-deepening humility and dependence on God.

The Apostle Paul is a good example. While he was used by God almost immediately after his conversion, it would take years and a series of painful serendestiny moments—shipwrecks, snake bites, beatings and imprisonments—to produce in him the humility needed to "finish the race."[41] Paul's own words reflect his decades-long descent into humility.

"Paul, an apostle—sent not from men nor by man, but by Jesus Christ and God the Father..."[42] This was how Paul described himself approximately fourteen years after his conversion.

---

37. Genesis 12

38. Genesis 37-50

39. Joshua 14:6-15

40. Exodus 7:7

41. 2 Timothy 4:7

42. Galatians 1:1

"For I am the least of the apostles..."[43] Paul declared twenty years after his conversion.

"...I am the least of all God's people..."[44] was Paul's self-assessment twenty-five years after surrendering to Christ.

And finally, "Christ Jesus came into the world to save sinners—of whom I am the worst,"[45] Paul conceded after thirty years as a Christ follower.

As time passed Paul grew in humility, something that allowed him to "press on to take hold of that for which Christ Jesus took hold of [him]".[46] What God called Paul to do was, by human standards, impossible. Even Jesus understood that "He [the Father] must become greater; I must become less."[47] And while becoming "less" can be a long and painful process for any believer, it ultimately prepares us to proclaim, like Paul: "I can do all things *through Christ* who strengthens me."[48]

Accepting God's timing has certainly been critical to realizing His plans for the ministry of Forward Edge. It took more than twenty years for Forward Edge to evolve from a short-term missions agency into a full-fledged relief and development organization. During our early years I felt like a fisherman pulling on the oars of a tiny rowboat. Today, I feel

43. 1 Corinthians 15:9

44. Ephesians 3:8

45. 1 Timothy 1:15

46. Philippians 3:12

47. John 3:30

48. Philippians 4:13

like the first mate on a three-masted schooner, with God's Spirit blowing in our sails.

Even this book, along with the memoir that preceded it, are the fruits of a long and sometimes painful "gestation period."

I first started writing my memoir, *Message in a Body*, in the late 1970s at the request of a major Christian publisher. They eventually decided not to pursue the project, and the manuscript bounced from one house to the next, until it landed in the hands of another top publisher. An editor there had me re-write the book, something that took months, and then offered me a contract.

But the contract never came. Before we could work out the details, this publisher was purchased by another house, and their senior editor decided to turn my book down. *Years* of moonlighting work had gone into this project, and now it seemed like the only people who'd ever read it were a handful of family and friends. I was devastated.

To make matters worse, two subsequent books I co-authored—one about a "coming world crisis" that never came; the other about a Central American president who was removed from office while we were proofreading the galleys—came to similarly inauspicious ends. Both made it into print, but, for obvious reasons, neither sold well.

Then, in 1982, God gave me the vision for Forward Edge. As the years passed and Forward Edge grew, my only writing projects were periodic newsletters and direct-mail appeals. I would not take on another book project for almost thirty years, when I was just shy of my sixtieth birthday.

Waiting on God had its benefits, though. When I dusted off the original *Message in a Body* manuscript written in the early '80s, I discovered that time had not only given me more to write about, but a cleaner and wiser heart. Gone were the judgments and self-righteousness of my younger self, replaced by—yes—a tad more humility. Years ago, I'd been devastated when my memoir was rejected. Now I am grateful it was never published.

This book, too, is the product of much time. Everything you've read in these pages, in fact—the importance of total surrender, of experiencing God's love, of responding the right way to hardships, of remaining flexible, of appreciating the unique call God has on each of our lives, of understanding and appreciating the role of serendestiny—is the byproduct of living for nearly forty years as a follower of Christ. Yes, I had some understanding of these things even as a new believer. But it took *time* to weave them into the fabric of being, to make them more than just biblically accurate information, but deeply held and hard-won *convictions*.

Finding and embracing God's best story for our lives is a process. And while God can and does use us wherever we are along the way, fully accomplishing His plans for us takes perseverance and what can seem at times like an unreasonable amount of patience.

I've know many believers who heard God's call early in their lives but had to wait decades before He sent them to fulfill it. For them, waiting was not something passive; it was an active and unwavering trust in a God who knew what was best for them, regardless of how long He took to reveal it.

One of my favorite stories about this kind of patience involves my longtime friends Jeff and Kris Thompson.

I first met Jeff and Kris at a Forward Edge conference in 1990. A twenty-something contractor from Seattle, Jeff was a Bible college graduate who had recently served on a mission team to Papua, New Guinea.

"I've felt a call to missions since Bible college," Jeff told me during my first conversation with him. "I'm not sure when God will send me, but I'm confident that day will come."

Over the years, I would periodically ask Jeff to facilitate Forward Edge mission teams, but as a busy father of three boys with a construction job, he could never break free. Kris, on the other hand, served on a Forward Edge team to Kosovo in 2000 and the following year on a team to New York City after 9/11.

It wasn't until 2002—more than ten years after I first met him—that Jeff was finally able to join Kris on her second trip to Kosovo. They would return twice more, and then in 2006, they *led* their first FEI team on an outreach to Mississippi after Hurricane Katrina.

It was around this time that Forward Edge received the grant from Murdock Trust. We already had volunteer field staff in the Gulf Coast, but now we had the means to strengthen and expand our team by hiring full-time staff. I decided to call Jeff.

"Wow, thanks, Joseph," Jeff replied, when I offered him the job. "I've got a big job I need to finish right now, but we'll definitely pray about it. Can I get back to you in a couple weeks?"

"Sure," I said. "Just call me when you're ready."

I turned off my phone and lifted Jeff and Kris up in prayer. The Hand of Serendestiny was clearly tapping on their shoulders, and I wondered how they would respond.

Two weeks later, Jeff called me back. "Kris and I are ready to accept your offer," he said, his voice charged with excitement. "I need to tie up a few loose ends, but we can probably be in the Gulf by the end of next month."

The Thompsons would spend more than two years in Mississippi and New Orleans, coordinating the work of over 1,000 short-term volunteers. When our work in the Gulf no longer required full-time field staff, I invited them to serve with FEI in Nicaragua. We'd launched a well-drilling project on the Atlantic coast—the poorest region in Latin America—and we needed someone to keep it on track.

The Thompsons accepted God's call once again, and have spent more than three years in Nicaragua. As a direct result of their efforts, hundreds of Nicaraguan villagers now have safe drinking water, and they are nearing completion of a home for more than one hundred at-risk children. In 2012, Jeff became director of all FEI community development projects and a member FEI's management team.

It took twenty-five years for Jeff's dream of becoming a missionary to materialize. He was barely twenty when God first called him; he was forty-five when he was finally sent. One can only speculate as to why it took so long. Perhaps God needed time to mold their characters. Or maybe it was just His way of bringing Himself more glory. Whatever the reason, it was their patience, and their embrace of serendestiny, that allowed them to discover and fulfill His plans for them.

The story of the Thompsons—like the stories of countless other Christ followers—powerfully reflects the oft-neglected truth that God may be slow, but He's never late. "…let us run *with perseverance* the race marked out for us," Paul the apostle exhorts in Hebrews 12:1. It's advice that often means the difference between a life of frustration and a life of fruitful service.

DISCUSSION STARTERS:

❯ On a scale of 1-10, with 10 = high and 1 = low, how would you rate your ability to be patient?

❯ Has impatience ever caused you to either "get ahead of God" or "stop running the race"?

❯ Read Isaiah 40:31. Can you think of a time when waiting on God eventually allowed you to "soar like an eagle"?

18

DENOUEMENT

....

"When in the dim beginning of the years, God mixed in man the raptures and the tears, And scattered through his brain that starry stuff, He said: "Behold! Yet this is not enough; For I must test his spirit to make sure That he can dare the vision and endure. I will withdraw my face, Veil me in shadow for a certain space, Leaving behind me only a broken clue —A crevice where the glory glimmers through, Some whisper from the sky, Some footprint in the road to track me by. I will leave man to make the fateful guess, To leave him torn between the no and yes, Leave him unresting 'til he rest in me, Drawn upward by the choice that makes him free—Leave him in tragic loneliness to choose, With all in life to win or to lose."

— Edwin Markham (1852 - 1940)

....

THE FRENCH WORD *DENOUEMENT* SPEAKS TO a deep need in the human heart. Webster defines the word as: "1. the final outcome of the main dramatic complication in a literary work; 2. the outcome of a complex sequence of events."

Like most people, I prefer my *denouements* rosy, with a neat little bow on top, gold if possible. But life doesn't always work out that way. As my friend Colonel Rogers used to tell volunteers while instructing them on the proper use of chainsaws: "People die."

On this side of heaven, we don't get answers to all of our questions. God doesn't respond as we'd hoped to all our prayers. And every step of faith doesn't lead to a God honoring success story.

But we *can* be sure of this: God's presence will never leave us, and nothing can separate us from His love. The outcome of every complex sequence of events won't be rosy. But however dark and inexplicable those events might be, we can always choose to bow our heads and pray this simple, life-giving prayer: "Lord, I don't understand. But I trust You."

JANUARY, 2010

"We need *solutions!*" The words of Haiti's Secretary of State reverberated in the air like the wail of a grieving widow. And the fact that he was staring right at me made my hair stand on end. In fact, everyone present—the mob of earthquake victims, the U.S. military contingent and the dais of dignitaries—was watching me, curious to hear what I would say. Almost a month since the earthquake, "solutions" were still in short supply.

Reminding myself that I'd done nothing to orchestrate the challenge that confronted me, I rose warily to my feet. "I know how much you and your families are suffering," I began, my eyes scanning the crowd of earthquake survivors. "And I certainly understand your need for food. We will do everything we can to help."

I glanced in the direction of the Secretary of State, and repeated my earlier endorsement. "Danny Jeune is a good man. If anything can be done to get him food, tarps and hygiene kits, I know they'll be put to good use."

Fully aware that my remarks fell short of solutions, I sat back down, flooded with feelings of remorse. Here I was being asked for answers, and all I'd come up with was my own appeal for help. I hoped that someday we could do more.

Two days later, Nick, Bob, Dan and I returned to the States. We were overwhelmed by what we'd seen and immediately started planning a response. We mobilized health-care professionals—doctors, nurses and EMTs—to provide emergency medical care. We also decided to recruit and send volunteers to assist the twenty thousand survivors squatting at Grace Village. A large Portland church—Solid Rock—would become our number one partner, providing funds to purchase temporary shelters and hundreds of short-term volunteers to help assemble them.

I phoned Danny to see how he was doing.

"Are you getting the resources you need?" I asked.

"It's amazing," he replied. "We're getting food, tarps, hygiene kits—everything we'd been hoping and praying for. The meeting with the Secretary of State got us on the radar of the UN, and now the resources are pouring in. I've even been asked to oversee emergency relief efforts for another 80,000 people! Please keep us in your prayers, Joe. And thanks so much for your willingness to help."

In the months and years that followed, Forward Edge would send more than 1,000 volunteers to Haiti. Colonel Rogers would spend three months coordinating our efforts in Jacmel, and we sent another man, Jeff Hartley, to coordinate our efforts in Carrefour. By the end of 2011, more than 300 health-care professionals had served with FEI in Haiti, most based out of a large Christian school in Port-au-Prince. In addition, Forward Edge teams—serving alongside local Haitians—distributed 50,000 meals at Grace Village, built nearly 100 temporary shelters, and removed more than 9,000 tons of rubble.

While undeniably tragic, the earthquake had proved a serendestiny moment that sparked an extraordinary outpouring of compassion. And like most serendestiny moments, it was also a doorway into new and unfamiliar territory.

In addition to providing emergency relief, Forward Edge pursued a long-term vision of partnering with Grace International to develop sustainable communities. It would take millions of dollars to realize these plans, but if God was in it, we felt confident—or at least hopeful—that He would provide. The Haitian government had given Grace several parcels of land, and another Grace partner, Engineering Ministries International

(EMI), sent teams of surveyors, architects and engineers to create site plans for these properties—plans that included not only permanent housing, but churches, schools, farm land and sites for income-producing businesses. We knew that if we merely built homes for earthquake victims without providing the means for them to support themselves, our efforts would be misguided. Did we really want to spend millions of dollars—money we had not yet raised—only to build *slums*?

We were also determined not to do things for Haitians that they could do for themselves. The last thing we wanted was to reinforce the cycle of dependence that had crippled Haiti for generations. Emergency relief was one thing; *empowering* people was something altogether different.

With this in mind, we made *job creation* our top priority. We conducted fundraisers on Portland radio stations to raise funds for chicken-breeding businesses. A million eggs a day were trucked into Haiti from the Dominican Republic—eggs that could easily be produced inside Haiti. Eggs were also the cheapest form of protein, and since most Haitian children were not getting their daily minimum requirement of protein, chicken-breeding seemed an ideal industry to support.

But challenges persisted. Funding family-run chicken businesses did not make financial sense when the cost of feed, medications and transportation wiped out most of the profits, leaving the breeders with little or nothing to support their families, let alone re-invest in their businesses.

What are You doing, Lord? we began to wonder. *We stepped out in faith and obedience, but keep running into roadblocks. Are You still with us?*

The story of our involvement in Haiti is still being written. By the time you read this book, I pray we'll have had another series of serendestiny moments to light our way. Because while the details may be unique to us, the experience is universal. Like any organization or individual seeking to do God's will, we had to follow Him into the unknown, unsure where He was leading or what the outcome would be.

You, too, may be somewhere in the valley between God's call and the mountaintop that someday reveals His plan. Or worse, you may be trudging—sad and fearful—through the forest of a serious testing, a thicket of unwelcome circumstances not anticipated or sought for.

This, my friend, is the landscape of serendestiny. It is the ancient tract where numberless pilgrims for millennia have had to "make the fateful guess...between the no and yes" left "in tragic loneliness to choose, with all in life to win or lose."

I pray you choose well.

"Do you think we'll see him, Dad?" Heather whispered, peering expectantly at the motionless waters of Dingle Bay, Ireland.

Over the years, my three children had heard Karen and I retell the story of the dolphin in Dingle's harbor. So when Kate left her American college to spend a year as an exchange student in England, my oldest daughter Heather and I decided to visit her—a trip that would include a brief tour of Ireland.

Again, we spent only a day in Dublin before driving to

Dingle, retracing the steps Karen and I had taken years earlier. We headed for the harbor and arrived just before dusk.

"Do you think we'll see him, Dad?" Heather repeated, her eyes fixed on the harbor.

"I don't know, Heather," I replied. "I hope so."

Several minutes passed with no sign of Fungi.

"Why don't we pray?" I finally suggested, half joking. I wanted Heather and Kate to have the same experience Karen and I had had, and if that required prayer, so be it.

"Lord, please let Fungi show up tonight," I whispered. "Please, Lord, *please.*"

Fifteen more minutes passed, as the Dingle lighthouse blinked in ten-second intervals. Then thirty minutes. Then sixty. But no Fungi.

At last, with the harbor blanketed by darkness, we returned to our rental car and headed back to town. For Kate and Heather, Fungi would remain just a character in a fanciful story their parents had told them. No matter how hard I prayed, the dolphin did not cooperate with my wishes. He had his own ideas, his own time frame, his own bright but unknowable agenda.

Somewhere, though, beneath the watery shroud of Dingle Bay, I knew he was present. Invisible. Majestic. Unrelenting. Ready to appear, whenever and however he saw fit. And that was enough.

DISCUSSION STARTERS:

❯ Read Hebrews 11:1 and 32-39. What do you think allowed these heroes of the faith to embrace God's call on their lives even though they died without receiving what was promised?

❯ How do you think "being sure of what [you] hope for and certain of what [you] do not see" can fill your life with purpose, and bring glory to God?

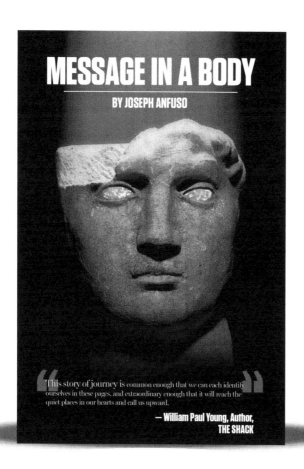

26977387R00107

Made in the USA
Columbia, SC
22 September 2018